ENDORSEMENTS

Angel Armies is an in-depth and exciting presentation of how we work with our heavenly helpers, the angelic forces, to accomplish God's will on earth. God bless you, Tim, for blessing the body of Christ with this book.

Bishop Bill Hamon
Christian International Ministries

We are living in the days when God is releasing angels on assignment for His people, and the Church needs to be prepared to co-labor with them. In *Angel Armies*, Dr. Tim Sheets presents a powerful, biblical viewpoint of how to apostolically cooperate with the heavenly host to bring God's Kingdom purposes to pass on planet earth. Every prophetically inclined believer should pore over this book to gain understanding and revelation as well as to avoid error concerning this very important supernatural realm.

Apostle Jane Hamon
Vision Church at Christian International

I have never met an individual who not only carried a powerful message but carried the heart of a true apostolic father like Apostle Tim Sheets. There are many teachers in the body of Christ, but Paul said, *"For though you might have ten thousand instructors in Christ, yet you do not have many fathers"* (1 Cor. 4:15 NKJV). I am beginning to understand that a man can give a word, but there is power to change your life when it comes from the heart of a true father.

Tim Sheets is a father to this generation, and what an opportunity to glean from the wisdom of many years walking with God, many years in ministry, but more importantly thousands of hours of study that has produced life-altering revelation. In a time when most have shunned the power of God and explained away the supernatural, Apostle Tim has been raised up in this hour to declare our help is on the way. God is truly releasing His angel armies upon the earth. You need this word from God so you can be positioned for heaven's greatest outpouring. This is a game changer for the body of Christ, because the ones who are for us are greater than those who are against us!

Mark Casto
Author, *When Misfits Become Kings*
Omega Center International
Mark Casto Ministries
Cleveland, Tennessee

The family of God is about to embark on a glorious new wave of Holy Spirit power and authority. Dr. Tim Sheet's book, *Angel Armies,* provides the motivation and instruction to better position you to participate in all God has planned in these end times. This bold, insightful teaching into the Kingdom of God and your role as an heir of salvation will resonate true to your heart. It is time now for the release of angel armies.

Doctors Bob and Audrey Meisner
TV Hosts, *MyNewDay*
Bestselling authors, *Marriage Under Cover*
New Day Ministries, Canada

What you hold in your hand is a written record of the scriptural and prophetic insights that God has given Dr. Tim Sheets regarding angel armies. Like thousands of believers around the world, I have been delighted in hearing Dr. Sheets share his unique insights on how God dispatches His angel armies as *"ministering spirits sent forth to minister for those who will inherit salvation"* (Heb. 1:14 NKJV). Now to have this revelation in written form is certainly a blessing for the body of Christ. Just as I did when Dr. Sheets shared these truths in our church, I wholeheartedly endorse this book as an encouraging treasure for every believer.

Mark W. Pfeifer
Author, *Alignment*
Senior Pastor, Open Door Church
Chillicothe, Ohio

I cannot recall when I have read a more encouraging book than *Angel Armies* written by my friend and ministry colleague, Dr. Tim Sheets!

It is hard to find very many books which declare, *"The greatest days in church history are not in its past; they are in the future."*

This book will greatly encourage the body of Christ and open up revelation concerning the Church's resources, which are too often forgotten or ignored, i.e., the angels of God, whom Dr. Tim labels "the Heir Force." He reminds us that angel armies are sent by God to minister to the saints and to assist the Church in releasing the power of the Holy Spirit to change the world.

This volume is well researched, biblically accurate, and theologically sound. It will provide us a much-needed apostolic and prophetic strategy in advancing the Kingdom of God in the 21st century and in our pursuit of spiritual awakening and reformation.

Use this book for personal spiritual growth, for conducting Bible studies, and in prayer gatherings. You will witness firsthand the courage meter go up in your life and in the lives of those who embrace the truths of this book.

Jim Hodges
Founder and president of the Federation of
Ministers and Churches International
Duncanville, Texas

Tim Sheets has an amazing revelation on the angelic that doesn't tickle your ears; it ratchets up your faith, courage, and action exponentially. You and I have a whole "heir force" behind us! I couldn't set this book down but had to devour it! I dare you to read it. Your faith will explode!

Barbara J. Yoder
Lead Apostle, Shekinah Regional Apostolic Center
www.shekinahchurch.org
www.barbarayoderblog.com

The revelation and apostolic declaration in this book contains pivotal modern-day marching orders for the body of Christ and speaks directly to the day and time we are now in.

Dr. Tim Sheets' insight into the angel armies and their strategic workings as revealed in this book bring an eye-opening acute definition to the angelic hosts and their activities as never before.

God has been preparing the Church for the greatest days in church history as Dr. Tim states, and this requires revelation that we must have in order to take part in the great collaboration of heaven and earth. I believe this book delivers that and chronicles the blueprint of heaven revealing the Father's strategy for the fulfilling of Revelations 11:15: *"The kingdoms of this world have become the kingdoms of our Lord."*

This book will no doubt be a faith classic for the modern-day church as well as a vital tool for establishing the Kingdom of God. I stand grateful for a genuine father in the faith and a consistent voice of truth as I have found in Dr. Tim Sheets.

Rev. Jen Tringale
Jen Tringale Ministries
Fort Worth, Texas
Author of *Your Defining Moment: When Time and Destiny Meet*

We are entering what is known as a "New Season of Awakening" in the Body of Christ. Many people call this the Third Great Awakening for the Church. I believe this is an age of Kingdom clashes! Dr. Tim Sheets has written one of the best books I have read, for the age ahead. This is a season when the Lord of Hosts, Lord Sabaoth, the God of the Armies, is aligning His troops in Heaven and on Earth. We must understand that we are not alone, and we could never win the war ahead depending upon our own weapons and capabilities. In *Angel Armies*, Apostle Tim clearly communicates the spiritual dynamic of the alignment of the angelic government in Heaven with the apostolic government on Earth. This is a *must-read* book for the times in which we are living. The promises and principles included in, and the benefits you will receive from reading *Angel Armies* will surpass most tools that you could acquire to help you during this time. This is a book that will prepare you for the future and help you see and be victorious in the clash of Kingdoms around you!

Dr. Chuck D. Pierce
President, Global Spheres Inc.
President, Glory of Zion Intl.

ANGEL
ARMIES

ANGEL
ARMIES

RELEASING *the* WARRIORS *of* HEAVEN

TIM SHEETS

DESTINY IMAGE® PUBLISHERS, INC.
P.O. Box 310, Shippensburg, PA 17257-0310
"Promoting Inspired Lives."

This book and all other Destiny Image and Destiny Image Fiction books are available at Christian bookstores and distributors worldwide.

Cover design by: Karen Webb

For more information on foreign distributors, call 717-532-3040.
Reach us on the Internet: www.destinyimage.com.

ISBN 13 TP: 978-0-7684-0874-4
ISBN 13 eBook: 978-0-7684-0875-1

For Worldwide Distribution, Printed in the U.S.A.
13 14 15/ 22 21 20

DEDICATION

To my wife, Carol, and to our children, Rachel (Mark) Shafer and
Joshua (Jessica) Sheets, and our five grandchildren—Madeline, Lily,
Jude, and Jaidin Shafer and Joelle Sheets, for all of their loving sup-
port and prayers; and to our Oasis Church family, who have provided
a base of support, encouragement, and intercession for the journey.
Our best days are in our present and in our future.

ACKNOWLEDGMENTS

Angel Armies has been a ten-year journey, and the journey was not taken alone. There are many to thank and I must begin with my wife, Carol, who not only has been along for the journey but whose persistent "nudges" to get this into writing kept the project alive. She has been involved every step of the way.

From the beginning of this process there has been prayer, encouragement, counsel, and practical help. I owe a huge thanks to Marie Fox, Katelyn Strack, and Cassandra Henderson, who went above and beyond to help us complete the manuscript. Transcribing, research, editing, proofreading—you endured! To Jennifer Peterson, Pam Roark, Brenda Stephens, and Rachel Shafer who all helped in the early stages when it was just a dream—thank you.

I also want to acknowledge Brad Herman for his input and advice, as well as the staff of Destiny Image for their expertise and encouragement.

To my brother, Dutch Sheets, and his wife, Ceci—thank you for sharing all the lessons and wisdom you have gained on your own path of authoring and publishing. Blessed to be related!

Oasis Church, I am honored to serve you and grateful for the intercession that has accompanied this process. Together we are better.

Above all, I am thankful for angel armies and the Captain of the Hosts, Lord Jesus. May the journey continue.

CONTENTS

FOREWORD

One of my favorite lines from the 1989 *Batman* movie comes from the Joker, played by Jack Nicholson. In the scene, Joker should have been angry and bemoaning the fact that Batman saved the damsel and escaped his clutches once again. Instead, however, he's impressed by and envious of Batman's many cunning tools—ingenious devices used to thwart his efforts and turn the tables on his devious plans. Rather than an angry tirade, Joker simply squawks out what actually concerns him the most, "Where does he get those wonderful toys?"

Sometimes, when listening to Tim teach, I feel a little like the Joker—impressed and envious. *Where does he get this stuff?* I squawk with a bedazzled smile.

Actually, I know where he gets it—he studies. Then he studies some more. And have I mentioned that he studies a lot? To be the best teacher, you have to be the best student. My brother, Tim, is both.

And he prays.

Prayer precedes and initiates revelation. Study produces knowledge, but study mixed with prayer births revelation. If you don't know the difference, you will shortly. You're about to be given remarkable and fascinating information. Though scholarly and deep, it will be anything but dry and boring; the insights will be exciting and life giving.

In fact, at times you will finish a paragraph or two only to find yourself thinking, *I need to read that again—slowly*. It won't be because you didn't understand it; it will simply be that you'll want to savor and digest the revelation more slowly and fully. Some things shouldn't be rushed. How do I know this will happen to you? Experience.

Angel Armies is the result of many years and hundreds of hours of research. I know because I've been goading Tim to write it for several of those years. I'm glad he waited...because he kept studying. And praying.

I'm also glad he waited until now because the timing is so right. Tim believes, as do many prophetic leaders, that we are moving into the greatest outpouring of the Holy Spirit in history. And he believes angels will play a significant role. I concur. And it will be helpful to know they're assisting and partnering with us.

As much as I believe in this human-angel partnership, however, I am very aware of the caution needed in approaching the subject. As with any element of the supernatural, "angel doctrines" can get a bit strange, and unfortunately some individuals have gotten into serious deception regarding them. Images, messages, assignments, and other "revelations" are sometimes attributed to angels when in reality they are conjured up from very active imaginations. Worse yet, other people have gained the information from deceiving demonic spirits, who are always looking for someone in whom to take advantage. Take comfort from the fact that this book is written by a true scholar and based on sound interpretation of Scripture.

Some may wonder why we need to understand and be more aware of angels and their roles. One obvious answer is because of the faith and confidence it produces. It's very motivating to know there are more for me than against me. I am much more inclined to face an enemy if I know I'll win!

It also is important to understand the role angels play in delivering messages. Whether Jacob, Daniel, or Joseph in the Old Testament or Peter or Paul in the New Testament, we are much more inclined to hear the message angels are delivering if we're alert to their presence and the role they play. We are also much less apt to be deceived by our own imaginations or evil spirits, thinking we're really hearing from angels, if we understand what Scripture teaches regarding the operation of these spirits sent from God. These are exactly the types of tools and insights you will find in this book.

You're about to read what will doubtless become one of today's textbooks on angels. Pastors will preach from it, teachers will use it in courses they teach, small groups will utilize it for their studies together, and individuals will devour its interesting content. Ultimately, this book will be translated into numerous languages; I have no doubt that *Angel Armies* will become a classic.

Now sit back and enjoy *Angel Armies*.

Dutch Sheets
Author, Apostle
Dutch Sheets Ministries
Dallas, Texas

INTRODUCTION

One of the greatest benefits God has given His church and heirs is angel assistance. Understanding their valuable and present help, supervised by Holy Spirit and balanced by Scripture, is fascinating to say the least. It is vital information for the believer in order to live a victorious Christian life. For more than ten years Holy Spirit has led me on a journey revealing how angels assist born-again believers. As I have pondered scripture after scripture in the Old and New Testament, I found myself saying often, "Why was I never taught this? Why didn't I know this? How could I have been raised in church all my life and not know how Holy Spirit and His angels assist the church?" I began to realize that emphasizing this awesome biblical truth was a part of my assignment. This book will detail my journey and how the Word was opened to me as He taught me the nature and work of angels.

I will never forget the afternoon I was in prayer when Holy Spirit spoke to me saying, "I will now lead the greatest move of God the world has ever seen. It will be similar to the outpouring on the Day of Pentecost in Acts chapter two." Then He added something that I was not expecting. "This time I will be coming with more of the Angel Armies." I knew He was revealing something to me that was so big, so important. Truly I was afraid to move. I simply sat by the lake where I was praying, thinking like Mary, mother of Jesus, saying from my heart, "Holy Spirit, show me what this means. Teach me. I'll study, I'll apply myself, but please show me what this means."

Holy Spirit, the awesome teacher Christ promised, began to teach me about angels. He led me through the Word, revealing the fifteen characteristics of an angel's nature, showing me their personality profile. This was something I had never thought about. Then He showed me what angels do. I was amazed at the dozens of things angels do for us. The Scriptures are filled with them. One of my favorite things was discovering how angels are assigned to believers, helping them fulfill their destinies. They even reveal and help pull from us potential we didn't even know God had put inside each one of us. I look forward to sharing with you in this book how angels have been briefed on your purpose from the day you were born.

One aspect of my study kept coming to the forefront. Angels are needed beings. God didn't make angels just to see what they would do. He didn't make them to just wander around the universe. No— they have great purpose. A part of that purpose is to assist the ministry of the church and the saints. I began to see that if the Godhead used angels to assist their ministry, and we see that often in the Scriptures, why then wouldn't we need them to assist us? They are very needed beings. It was God's idea to have them assist us.

As Holy Spirit led me into this area of enlightenment, He gave me a statement I have quoted time and time again. On another day out at the lake, my favorite place to pray, Holy Spirit spoke this phrase of great hope to me. It will lead us into the teaching of this book...

"The greatest days in church history are not in your past, they are in your present and your future!"

chapter one

VORTEX FIRE

Preface

There are times we must pause and reflect upon what the Holy Spirit is trying to communicate to us through prophetic words and spiritual experiences. Before we take a comprehensive look at the makeup of heaven's angelic hosts, I want to share with you some of the prophetic words that have been given in my Ohio church, as well as to my wife and me personally. Not only can these words be applied corporately, but they also provide the background for my understanding of the workings of the angel network.

Over the years, I have noticed that people tend to receive prophetic words, but then put them on the shelves of their lives, not knowing what to do with them. This is not God's intention for His messages. He means for us to understand and grab hold of them in faith. Prophetic words are not meant to be hidden or confusing; they are meant to plant seeds in our lives that bring forth a harvest as we carefully water them with prayer and tend them with keen action. We must take prophetic words, test them against Scripture, and then meditate upon them, being ready to implement them into our lives when the proper season arrives. We must refresh ourselves by personal remembrance of these words so that they build in intensity within our hearts and minds, lest we let them fall stagnant by the wayside. Simply said, if we do not use them, we will lose them.

I am excited to share with you some of the things God has spoken through the prophets of our day, because these prophecies stand the test of time. Recurring themes are woven so evidently between many of them, it is obvious that God is up to something and is trying to get His message across to us. I also believe it is important that we hear and re-hear prophetic words because they spark the faith needed to make a course correction in our lives as we see the pieces of the puzzle coming together. Prophetic words are visions for the future, strategies to be implemented, or prayer points on which to intercede until they come to fruition on earth. In the upcoming pages, you will be reminded of prophetic statements that we are to judge according to Scripture and, having proved them accurate, to obey.

The Third Great Awakening

We consistently receive the prophetic word that we are entering into a season of fresh Holy Spirit fire. When my church participated in forty days of prayer and worship (which extended another eighty days!), this word came up nightly. People all over our state began to ask for fresh fire of the Holy Spirit to spread across the country. Because the Holy Spirit has restated and reemphasized this, we recognize it is His desire for the body of Christ, for those who will choose to obey Him. He wants to breathe fresh anointing on this remnant—not just to be a blessing to those within the four walls of the church, but also to empower believers to be Kingdom ambassadors on the earth. Believers should be so saturated with the Holy Spirit that wherever they go, those they come in contact with are touched by the life-giving power of the Holy Spirit.

I am reminded of a vision I saw of two submarines—one was a very old submarine, such as we would have seen in the first half of the twentieth century. That old submarine was submerging under the water and I heard the Holy Spirit say, *"That is the Charismatic movement. It is now submerging into the culture it once ruled."* I then saw another submarine coming up out of the water, one of our new nuclear Triton submarines. It was just breaking the surface when I heard the Holy Spirit say, *"That is His remnant, New Testament church. It will now emerge from the culture to rule and reign."* Now, for that to happen, the church must be endued with power from on high, filled and refilled with the Holy Spirit. There must be a fresh fire and a fresh wind bringing forth a fresh anointing for us to live under. The anointing of the old season is not going to carry us forward to permeate and saturate a culture with God's life-changing love and power. To rule and reign in life through Christ as Romans 5:17 says, the church must emerge from the culture with something more real, more powerful, and more enticing to those who are lost. The time for this is not in the future. It is not around the corner. The time for this is right now.

The season of the Third Great Awakening has now begun. God is giving many prophetic words about this, paired with confirming signs that cannot be ignored or denied. We must prepare ourselves individually and corporately to receive the Holy Spirit's presence and power. We must dedicate our earthen vessels to be afresh and anew—not living our lives as we always have. We cannot make God's priorities another line on our to-do lists. Instead, we should realize that God's activity is reality and our lives should ebb and flow in the river of His Holy Spirit. We must prepare our regions, bathing them in prayer. We cannot continue to treat those in our neighborhoods, our cities, our metropolitan areas, our states, and so forth, as if they are out of reach. With love, grace, forgiveness, and open arms, we should accept them as people created and loved by God Himself. As we do this, we make the cause of Christ truly known. We extend His Kingdom by being His hands and feet on the earth.

We must prepare an Upper Room over our lives, our families, our cities, our states, and our countries to call down God's glory. When we get in touch with what God is doing, He leads us to move in timing only He could have planned. For example, my church participated in an event called the Prophetic Summit, the culmination of forty days of prayer and fasting. During the Friday night service of this event, it came to my attention that the date was a special one. It was on that same date that Egypt dethroned their pharaoh, King Mubarak. In Scripture, Egypt typifies bondage or captivity in darkness. The very fact that the Prophetic Summit event landed on this very day is nothing short of a sign of confirmation signaling a new move of deliverance and an emergent rule over the culture. In addition to this, the event also landed on the date of Moses' birth and death. The chance of all of the events occurring on the same date surely shows that God is releasing a mighty deliverance!

There Were Angels

I am reminded of a trip I took to Jacksonville, Florida, to minister at a church there. I was about a half hour late to the service when my flight landed and I finally arrived. Worship leader Rick Pino and his band were leading the congregation in praise as I walked in. It was evident from the moment I entered that high places were being reached and God's supernatural activity was stirring there. As I walked from the back to the front of the auditorium, I began to see flashes of light going back and forth across the congregation. I stopped in my tracks because, as I have taught, that refers to angelic activity. Angels were moving all around the auditorium, ministering to God's people.

At Pentecost, the Holy Spirit came with His heavenly Hosts, who appeared as flames of fire and settled upon each person present in the

Upper Room. Under the direction of the Holy Spirit in that Upper Room, the Hosts were ministering and delivering fresh, consecrating fire. I saw these flashes, these ministering angelic spirits, mere hours after I had been in Ohio declaring that the fresh fire of God was coming and sharing my prophetic vision about the submarines. I remember pausing in the aisle before I went forward, saying, "God, this is so big. Help me not to miss this. God, I don't want to be on the bench; I want to be a player. I want to be in the game. I don't want to sit this out."

The next morning began as the worship leader opened with a song to gather everyone together and prepare their minds for receiving mode. My brother, Dutch Sheets, opened the service in prayer. I stood there on the front row, getting ready to minister, when I saw, off to the right, a group of angels. To the left there was a group of angels stationed as well. They were angel warriors. I looked up and saw angel warriors stationed everywhere!

Of course, this captured my attention. It was even more spectacular to me because this had happened a few months prior in Rochester, New York, where I had seen two bands of angels on each side of those who had been called to the altar. Cindy Jacobs had requested that all teenagers and young adults up to the age of thirty come up to the front. As she began to pray over them, she called Dutch and me to help her pray over them as well. While we were praying, I heard, called out from behind me, "Mahanaim." I know exactly what *Mahanaim* is because I teach about it. Of course, God knew that that word would grab my attention and I would recognize it meant the Angel of the Lord who accompanies the apostolic assignment on my life. Finally I looked to see who was yelling, "Mahanaim." To my surprise, there was nobody behind me. I began to shake internally. Genesis 32 describes Jacob returning to Bethel to meet his brother Esau. He was concerned that Esau would kill him and his children, because he had stolen his birthright years before. When he returned to Bethel, he saw two camps, or groups, of angels standing on either side of his children, guarding them from Esau. Jacob named that place "Mahanaim," which means "the place of two camps" (Strong, H4266).

Back to the meeting in Jacksonville: I remembered what I had seen in New York and what I had read in Genesis 28. I saw the same thing and I knew the Holy Spirit was using the angels to protect what He is doing with the coming generation—particularly that night, what He was doing with the youth in that church. The church in Jacksonville had 1,500 students in their school who were learning to be cultural reformers. Many of this group were gathered at the altar, fired up and ready to receive from the Lord. I asked the Lord if He wanted me to share what I saw. As I stood there, thinking it through, Dutch got up to open in prayer. His opening line was, "God be the God of Bethel today." Remember from Genesis 28 that Bethel is Mahanaim's spot. I jumped up during Dutch's opening prayer, grabbed the microphone, and began to declare how the Holy Spirit is coming with His angels, that He is synergizing the coming generation with the older generation in the Third Great Awakening. Pastor Zink, the senior pastor of the Jacksonville church, stood and began to pray for spiritual fathers to be released to steward the coming generation, but not to control them. As the flow of the Spirit continued, I began to pray that spiritual fathers, who would so desire the coming generation to exceed them in wisdom and influence, would begin to use all of their influence, strategy, and knowledge to push the coming generation into their destiny.

The Vortex

As soon as I finished praying, Dutch said he heard the word *vortex*. "God says He is now coming as a vortex," he declared. A vortex is a mass of liquid with whirling or circular motion—a whirlpool. It is a spin or whirl of activity from which it is hard to escape. In other words, it spins so fast you are drawn into the center. *Vortex* also means tornado or spinning whirlwind—even a whirling mass of flames. They embody a rush of exciting, rapid changes that have an absorbing effect, a constant round of excitement or pleasure. In other words, you get caught up in a vortex.

I heard the worship leader say the word "shoutphesy." I thought to myself, does "shoutphesy" mean to prophesy really loudly? So I asked Rick Pino, who was standing beside me. He told me he did not hear the worship leader say that. I found out later that no one heard him say it! Not yet convinced, I asked the worship leader personally, only to find out he did not say it at all. Regardless, at that moment, I knew I heard to "shoutphesy," so I began to shout the words, "Come as a vortex! Come as a vortex!" It was stirring so deeply within me that I could not contain it.

I have now had two encounters with *Mahanaim*, seeing them surround, as guards, the next generation. Back in my own church in Ohio, we had a guest worship leader for a Sunday night service on the particular night I am about to describe. From the very beginning of that service, I could sense that visible angelic activity was going to take place. Sure enough, just as I had seen in New York and in Florida, the worship leader called for the young people to come up on the platform. I was immediately reminded of the *Mahanaim* I had seen the last two times this had happened. Just as I expected, I looked up and saw a band of warrior angels on both sides of the kids on the platform. It was the *Mahanaim*. This next generation had the angels' undivided attention, their eyes being riveted on the kids as they stood guard over them.

For whatever reason that night, the guest worship leader lay down on the platform. It just so happened that I had lain down on the platform that morning in the earlier service. I never do that. In fact, in thirty-one years of ministry, I had never done that! However, when I was talking about the kind of determination it would take to bring forth purpose and awakening, I lay down right in the middle of my sermon. Now, this guest worship leader did the exact same thing. I remember watching him and thinking that it was no coincidence. While he was lying down, he began to exhort us to press deeper into the Lord. I could hardly believe what happened next. He stood up and said, "I know this may sound unusual, but I hear the Lord saying that the Holy Spirit is coming to Ohio like a vortex." He did not know about the previous words that had been given about vortexes. He did not know that I had ministered to my congregation with those words. God was confirming this message again, saying that He is coming like a vortex of fire.

I have now seen this same thing repeat itself three times—in Rochester, New York; Jacksonville, Florida; and in Ohio. Obviously, with three clear confirmations, the Holy Spirit and His angels are moving to bring the coming generation into a Great Awakening through revival fire. A mighty move of the Holy Spirit is continuing to train and release these young believers so that they can help steward revival. Just as the prophet Joel said, this younger generation will prophesy. They will dream God's dreams. They will see God's vision. They will run with passion and fuel the passion of others. The older generation needs the fire the younger generation has and will continue to gain; however, the younger generation desperately needs the older generation's wisdom. It takes both groups, working together, to run with the Holy Spirit, to run with His remnant and with the angels.

Before any of these vortex prophecies[1] came forth, a man in my church prophesied that a hurricane wind was coming. It would fill entire states. This, of course, aligns exactly with what God is saying—that He is coming as a vortex! These vortex descriptions parallel Pentecost. A swirling mass of fiery anointing is coming like a whirlwind, accompanied by angelic activity, to God's remnant warriors. The wind of God spinning like a tornado is drawing us into His presence. A vortex of Holy Spirit fire is drawing believers, absorbing them. Millions are going to feel it. A rush of excited, rapid change is about to happen—change in church as usual, change in the culture, and change in America. It will be a round of constant excitement and pleasure. The mighty wind turbines of heaven are creating a vortex, as a spinning wheel spins in the middle of another wheel. Ezekiel 1:16 talks about this. The voice of God is speaking out and is clearly being heard, a vortex of anointing, of wind, of fire—a vortex coming to change, excite, and amass power!

NOTE

1. See Appendix: Prophecies of Confirmation, page 213.

chapter two

THE HOLY SPIRIT
AND ANGELS OF FIRE

Caesar Creek Lake is not far from my house. I have gone there to pray and seek the Lord for years now. In the fall of 2003, I was there again at one of my favorite places way back in the woods, facing a waterfall. As I asked Holy Spirit to clarify direction for the church, an amazing download began. Holy Spirit talked to me about another Pentecost He would soon steward upon the earth. He revealed that a new move of God would soon begin, a move that He described as an "awakening surge greater than the world has ever seen." He also revealed how His angels would assist, stating very clearly, "*This time I am coming with far more of the angel armies.*" To say He had my undivided attention would be an understatement. I was not expecting that statement at all.

As I sat pondering what was being said, Holy Spirit then branded a phrase into my spirit that I have declared hundreds of times since. It was as though He carved it into my DNA. He said, "*The greatest days in church history are not in its past, they are in its future.*" The significance of that statement was enormous. Something greater than any move of

God's Kingdom in history would now surge. Greater Kingdom power than has ever been seen will now flow from Christ's New Testament church. Enlightenment came that there is now an alignment of heaven's Angel Army with the Remnant Warrior Army and with what I now call the War Eagle Army from the coming generation. They will now synergize under Holy Spirit supervision to demonstrate that the Kingdom of God is present and functioning in great power.

From that very special day, Holy Spirit led me through the Scriptures, teaching me about His Angel Army. I was captivated by the revelation as, month after month, more was revealed. Yes, I knew angels were real, but they were not on my radar as Holy Spirit was now teaching. Awareness began to come of one of the greatest benefits to God's heirs—angel assistance. After months of research and study, the picture was now even clearer: "*The greatest days in church history are not in its past, they are in its future.*" Holy Spirit would supervise the greatest movement of the Kingdom of Heaven and it would happen in my time. I knew that this movement would move. It is meant to move. It is "move-meant," propelled by supernatural power. I knew that angel armies were behind this movement and that hell has never faced anything like it, nor have the remnant warriors. Holy Spirit is now marshaling His armies to change history.

Toward the end of this season of Holy Spirit training, He began to confirm His calling on my life. Back at the lake again, I heard Him say, "A part of your assignment in My new campaign is to deploy My angel army with bold decrees from Christ's heirs. Make decrees of faith a priority in your sphere of authority." I was also prompted continually: Discern your times and declare what is discerned.

Discerning Our Times Properly

We are living in the end times. The war that rages in the spirit world has intensified, as all attacks move toward the culmination of the future battle at Armageddon. As we see this increased kingdom activity, it is vital that we discern what is happening and know what our correct response to it should be.

In 1 Chronicles 12:32, the sons of Issachar both discerned the times and gained understanding of what Israel ought to do. In following their example of searching the season out, I feel it is vital to provide pertinent doctrinal foundations to help us discern the times in which we now live. Foundational truths add credibility to current kingdom activity and thus activate greater faith and confidence within us. They simultaneously refresh and refocus us.

To begin, let us examine the Hebrew roots of some words that will be important as we learn to discern the time:

- *Biynah* (understand): knowledge, wisdom, insight, intelligence (Strong, H998)

- *Eth* (times): the proper time or right season for an event to happen (Strong, H6256)

- *Yada* (know): to perceive, to anoint to see clearly, to inform, or to reveal; knowledge gained through the senses (to sense); to distinguish between options (Strong, H3045)

- *Asah* (ought to do): to execute, work, create or build; to prepare; describes God's creative activities (our implication is to prepare for God's activities) (Strong, H6213)

- *Rhema* words: Holy Spirit revealed revelation and enlightenment from the Scriptures

Understanding the Hebrew roots of these words prepares us for the release of revelation and *biynah* understanding. Remembering and meditating on such teaching, as well as the prophetic words we've received, allows *asah* to happen. It gives us intelligence and wisdom, revealing the appropriate time and action for an event that has come into season. It anoints us with perception to sense and distinguish the proper option so that it can be executed in work, and so that we can appropriately prepare for the release of God's creative activity into a "happening." In other words, past teachings and prophetic words coupled with present understanding of the times is vital for wisdom to flow and vision to be carried out at the right time.

It is time we rethink teachings, rethink prophetic words, in order to refocus our attention and increase wisdom for the now. This activates faith and confidence, giving us wisdom and intelligence for this season of God's creative activity.

Power!

In Acts 1 and 2, we read the last promise Jesus made to His disciples—indeed, the last statement He made before ascending into heaven. He prophesied the coming of the Holy Spirit. It was the appropriate time for Him to come; it was the *eth,* so they would be filled with power from on high.

When we speak of this kind of power, we should keep the word *dunamis* in mind. Although this is the root of the English word *dynamite, dunamis* power does not mean dynamite in and of itself. Rather, *dunamis* is the release of energy when something is lit and then explodes. It is a power capable of anything (Strong, G1411). In Acts 1:4 and 8, Jesus told His disciples not to leave Jerusalem until the Holy Spirit came and filled them. He was giving them this type of power to be His witnesses in Jerusalem (their city), Judea (their region), Samaria (heathen areas), and to the uttermost parts of the world.

The 120 believers, who gathered in the upper room following this instruction, were used to facilitate the new Kingdom campaign Christ wanted to release on earth. A campaign is a series of connected activities to get or do something, organized action to obtain a purpose, or a series of related military operations. Those who run for the office of president are said to be conducting political campaigns. In other words, they are organizing and acting to obtain their purpose. They are connecting their activities and workers to get something done. We, as believers, must be open and yearning for the power of the Holy Spirit to operate through our lives to extend the Kingdom of God on the earth, as did the 120 in the upper room, so that a new campaign can be carried out.

The Kingdom of God on Earth

The Kingdom of God is a spiritual realm extended on the earth in at least three ways—through the New Testament church that trains its saints, through the Holy Spirit who is one with Christ and the Father, and through the organized network of potentially billions of angels encamped around the earth, of which Christ is the leader.

Colossians 1:18 and 2:10 name Christ as head over every power and authority, which includes all principalities and dominions. He is the preeminent one; He is above all powers, might, and dominions. This refers to both angelic and demonic powers. There are demonic principalities and dominions trying to rule geographical areas. We are told in Ephesians 6:12 to bind such forces. Likewise, as described in Colossians 1 and 2, God has His own principalities, powers, and dominions at work. We should always remember that the kingdom of darkness simply counterfeits God's organized Kingdom in operation and rank.

There are millions of these angel warriors, fellow servants who are assisting us. Hebrews 12:22 says, it is *"an innumerable company of angels"* (NKJV). Only one third of the angels fell when Lucifer rebelled (see Rev. 12:4). That leaves two thirds of the angels left on our side unless God has created more angels. This means there are far more angels for us than fallen angels against us. It is at least two to one. That should add to the confidence of the overcomers, the remnant warriors. The word *remnant* simply refers to a small portion or a small percentage of the whole. Only a small portion of the church is really going to follow Christ on this end time campaign assignment. Most Christians today are nominal; they are in name only. They are not going to take part in this campaign.

The Natural Number Is Not the Kingdom Number

Sometimes in the natural realm we are very outnumbered. Sometimes the odds against us are incredibly high off the charts. There are some today who say you will never see an awakening or revival in the United States, because the odds are just too high. Sometimes the number in the natural realm looks impossible. But the natural number is not the Kingdom number! The Kingdom number is overwhelmingly in our favor. We've got to understand that. God is with us, Holy Spirit is with us, Messiah the Breaker goes before us, and millions of His angels are standing with us to implement strategy, plans, and laws to protect, to steward the resources, and to enforce covenants. In 2 Kings 6 the prophet Elisha and his servant found themselves surrounded by the Syrian army. They were incredibly outnumbered by the army and its war chariots, and Elisha's servant cried out to Elisha in 2 Kings 6:15, *"What shall we do?"* Elisha's response was, "Relax. There's more on our side than on their side." So Elisha's servant takes a head count—"one, two." Two was the natural number, but it wasn't the Kingdom number. Elisha prayed, "Lord, open his eyes." And when his servant's spiritual eyes were opened, he saw that the hillsides were filled with God's angel army. Horses, chariots of fire, and angels arrayed for battled surrounded them.

God gave miraculous victory in the face of overwhelming odds. Is the remnant number enough to see the greatest days in church history? Is the remnant number enough to see a worldwide revival? Is it enough to change this nation? Yes, because the natural number is not the Kingdom number. There are far more with us than with our adversary. God the Father, God the Son Jesus, the Holy Spirit, and millions of His angels are on our side. If the remnant will step forward into battle, though we see odds that are too great for us we will see the mighty army of the Kingdom of God come to our rescue. The shock and awe is not on the natural side, it is on the spiritual side. Far more than enough sides with us to give us victory.

The Angel Army

Joshua 5 recounts Christ's appearance to Joshua as he prepared to conquer Jericho:

> *Now it came about when Joshua was by Jericho, that he lifted up his eyes and looked, and behold, a man was standing opposite him with his sword drawn in his hand, and Joshua went to him and said to him, "Are You for us or for our adversaries?" He said, "No; rather I indeed come now as captain of the host of the Lord." And Joshua fell on his face to the earth, and bowed down, and said to him, "What has my lord to say to his servant?" (Joshua 5:13-14 NASB)*

In Hebrew, the word *hosts* is translated as *tsebaah*, which means warriors or soldiers organized for military service and equipped for war (Strong, H6635). The Lord's hosts, therefore, are a mass of angelic beings. This scripture makes it clear that there is a very real and organized angelic army. We often unconsciously think of angelic beings as imaginary or having little purpose, but you can see by now that this is far from the truth! They are created to carry out God's plans under the command of Christ Himself. They are mobilized by

His words, including those spoken forth by the saints. Psalm 103:20 (NLT) says, *"Praise the Lord, you angels, you mighty ones who carry out his plans, listening for each of his commands."* This means they listen and respond to the words of God that we speak (including Holy Spirit-inspired prophetic words and decrees of faith) organizing, fighting, and campaigning to bring them to pass. They are heavenly warriors.

This angel army does what armies do. What is it that armies do?

- Guard and protect a king and his kingdom

- Guard the inhabitants of the kingdom

- Implement the king's strategies, plans, and laws

- Protect kingdom boundaries (patrol the borders)

- Enforce the king's jurisdiction (where his authority reaches)

- Steward the king's resources or the kingdom's resources

- Facilitate and enforce covenants (whatever a king decrees)

- Keep weapons and weapon systems in operating condition

- War against threats to the kingdom

- Protect and assist a king's family (heirs)

Not only do heavenly warriors carry out God's words and commands, they also assemble around worship. They set ambushes against the enemies of God, including principalities, might, and dominions. We are told about this in 2 Chronicles 20 when Jehoshaphat, all of Judah, and the inhabitants of Jerusalem worshiped the Lord and gave their battle against Ammon, Moab, and Mount Seir to Him. God led them into victory through His own plans and commands as their recognition of His ability and worship prepared the way.

The Trinity and the New Campaign

In John 14:16, Jesus refers to the Holy Spirit as His other self, another comforter. Jesus said, *"And I will pray the Father, and he shall give you another Comforter, that he may abide with you for ever."* The word *allos* means "one of the same kind or quality or one of a pair" (Strong, G243). Jesus says here that the Holy Spirit would be sent to pair up with us, to be with us and in us. In that same chapter, Jesus said, *"If you had known Me, you would have known my Father also; and from now on you know Him and have seen Him"* (John 14:7 NKJV). These verses show that the Father, the Son (Jesus), and the Holy Spirit are one and the same.

Knowing this concept of the Trinity is vital because it brings clarification concerning when the Holy Spirit came at Pentecost—when He came with the Hosts of Heaven, the *tsebaah*. Remember, the *tsebaah* is the mass of angelic beings organized for military service and equipped for war. The Holy Spirit is also the head of the angel network, being one and the same with the Father and with Jesus. Acts 2:3 says, *"Then, what looked like flames or tongues of fire appeared and settled on each of them"* (NLT). Angels came with the Holy Spirit to minister fire from God's altar upon the 120 gathered in the upper room. They came to prepare and empower Christ's followers for the new campaign, for the transition of seasons in which they were living.

It is important to recognize Jesus as One who issued orders for a new campaign on earth in the first two chapters of Acts. His purpose in the upper room was to unify His church and cause them to participate in the empowerment delivered by His Holy Spirit. When we talk about Pentecost (Holy Spirit baptism), we are not simply focusing on the personal blessing or refreshing it brings. Certainly, the baptism of the Holy Spirit is about something much bigger than you or me. In the days of Pentecost, a new move of God was about to begin. The saints needed to be prepared and empowered to be

Kingdom extensions on the earth, for the King Himself was issuing the order. These 120, filled with divine empowerment from the Holy Spirit, turned the world upside down. They first affected their city, then their region, followed by heathen areas, and ultimately the uttermost parts of the earth. All of this was made possible because they recognized they were living in a new season that required mighty exploits.

Today's Pentecost

Like the days of Pentecost, the angel activity happening now is certainly ushering in another campaign unlike anything before in church history. Remember the definition of campaign: a series of connected activities to get or do something, organized action to obtain a purpose, or a series of related military operations. The Holy Spirit is organizing Kingdom extensions to obtain heavenly purposes, preparing for His activity and the biggest move of God in history. It is now time for the Third Great Awakening—the revival prophesied Joel. In Joel 2:25, the Lord promises to restore the years the locust have eaten away. He will restore our last harvest!

In this new campaign, the young and the old are going to participate together and operate with a transgenerational anointing. A new outpouring of the Holy Spirit is beginning with fresh anointing for members of the remnant. Although 500 people were told to go to that upper room, only 120 did. The remaining 380 had something better to do. Only those who will do what He said (the remnant) are qualified for this new anointing.

Holy Spirit is also coming to energize the remnant by releasing fresh anointings on the fivefold ministry—apostles, prophets, evangelists, pastors, and teachers. They must be refreshed and fired up for the new campaign. The calling is similar to that in Acts 1 and 2—extend Christ's Kingdom locally, regionally, and worldwide. Angels have come with Holy Spirit to assist in making that happen. They are working to shift the church into harvest mode. Can the world be turned upside down again? Yes. Just as Joshua and the people of God shifted from forty years of wilderness wandering into their promised land assisted by the host of angels, the *tsebaah*, just as the early church shifted from the Old Testament mindset to a New Testament power-filled Kingdom mindset assisted by the *tsebaah*—so it is today. We are now shifting into a new campaign of King Jesus, and we will likewise be assisted by the same *tsebaah*. The charismatic movement is over. It is now time for the apostolic campaign of King Jesus on this earth. Multitudes in the valley of decision are going to be brought in. Harvests are going to be restored sevenfold. A new move of the Holy Spirit is coming to the New Testament churches, and the angel army network is assisting in empowering the remnant to participate. As the Holy Spirit is organizing a new campaign to obtain God's purposes, His workers, saints, and the angelic network are to yield in full obedience to prepare and participate.

The Holy Spirit, Angels, and Fire

In Acts 2, we see Holy Spirit supervising angels who minister fresh fire. This is now happening in our times and it will accelerate. We must understand what was happening then, so we can know what is happening now. Hebrews 1:14 says, *"Are they* [angels] *not all ministering spirits, sent forth to minister for them who shall be heirs of salvation?"* We are the heirs of salvation. Notice it says they have been sent and they are ministering. Psalm 104:4 tells us God *"maketh his angels spirits; his ministers a flaming fire."* That is repeated in Hebrews 1:7. Let us examine the original Greek for some key words.

- *Leitourgos* (minister): a servant or a worshiper of God (Strong, G3011)

- *Phlox*: flame; a flash, blaze, or tongue of fire; lightning (Strong, G5395)

- *Poieo*: to make; to cause or to endow someone with a certain quality (Strong, G4160)

God makes His ministers a flaming fire. These are His servants and could include angels or born-again men and women on the earth. His servants are those who worship and serve God Himself, not just the fivefold ministry of apostles, pastors, teachers, prophets, and evangelists. Everyone who is born again is supposed to be one of God's ministers. This tells us that God wants every born-again believer ablaze for Him! He wants fresh fire blazing forth from your life as you burn with His glory and presence.

Acts 2:3 says on the day of Pentecost, cloven tongues of fire sat upon everyone in the upper room. All 120 had a flame over them, a cloven tongue of fire. Now remember that a divine shift was taking place as the church was transitioning to a different level. It was moving from the old covenant to a new level of authority and ministry. When that shift began, cloven tongues of fire, accompanied by the Holy Spirit, sat upon them. Angels ministered this fire to each believer so they would be empowered for the new campaign. Angels accompanying Holy Spirit were firing up the saints to move. This was to be a fired-up movement. The key to any movement is movement. Holy Spirit and His angels were clearly saying, *"Fire up and move!"*

This is what has been happening in recent times with increased angelic activity. Angels are even now ministering to help release a fresh outpouring of the Holy Spirit. One of their assignments is to bring fresh fire to believers under Holy Spirit supervision, to spiritually set them on fire. Ezekiel 1:13 begins this doctrine by describing angels as having the appearance of burning coals of fire, like the appearance of lamps that went up and down among the living creatures. The fire was bright with lightning shooting out from it. The angels appeared as flashes of light, or *pur*, cloven tongues of fire. The New Living Translation says that the living beings looked like brilliant torches, as though lightning was flashing back and forth among them. *The Bible in Basic English* says that between the living beings it looked as if flames were chasing after each other across burning coals of fire. This is exactly what it looked like on the day of Pentecost as bright fire flashed on top of the 120 believers! What was happening? Angels were ministering fresh fire from God's altar upon them. The angel network was accompanying the Holy Spirit, the other "self" of Christ, assisting in shifting the church to a new level of ministry.

Conclusion

I remember when God first started teaching me about angels and I would often see flashes of light everywhere. I now know that is a sign by which we can discern angelic activity. In Isaiah 6:6-7, Isaiah said that a seraph flew with a live coal in his hand, which he had taken with tongs from the altar. When the coal touched Isaiah's mouth, his iniquity was taken away and his sin was purged. Spiros Zodhiates, a Greek scholar, used this poignant description: "the Hebrew word *seraph* means a winged angel that appears as a brilliant glowing flame of fire." This gives us the mental picture of angels flying with live coals at Pentecost. The Holy Spirit, accompanied by the angel network, came to baptize the church in power and fresh fire. The assignment of those angels was to "fire up," or impassion, the people of God. This is still a major purpose for angelic activity today.

It is time for a new outpouring. It is time for the church to receive fresh power from on high. It is time for fresh fire upon all believers. It is time for a divine shift to take the church to new levels. It is time for the apostles and believers to begin affecting their regions with the Gospel, as angels under Holy Spirit supervision network with the church. They are moving now upon fresh Holy Spirit winds to assist the saints to do the same works Jesus did. They are flashing about as lightning. They are striking the enemies of King Jesus. Angels are bringing coals from the altar to cleanse iniquity and purify the people of God. They are ambushing hell's forces. They are acting on prophetic words. They are enforcing the decrees of the saints based on Scripture. They are pushing out principalities, powers, might, and dominions from the dark side that have organized against our King. They are helping to organize the new Kingdom of Heaven event that is taking place now. Angels are at work releasing God activity into the remnant. They are working the harvest with us. They are assisting the Third Great Awakening that has now begun. They are connecting people, places, and activities through the Holy Spirit's campaign. They are assisting in the return of stolen property, sevenfold. They are connecting for miracles, building and activating God's wonders, creating and giving Holy Spirit signs—all clearly revealing confirmations!

We are entering into the days of Christ's power evidenced in and through His remnant. There has never been a campaign like this one. The Synergy of the Ages and the Ancient of Days is behind it. Angel armies are behind it. The Holy Spirit is rising in unprecedented ways. It is the appropriate time to combine the efforts of heaven and earth under Holy Spirit supervision into a New Testament fiery explosion that the gates of hell cannot prevail against. This explosion of *dunamis* power will see millions saved. It will harmonize the generations, causing them to march with determination and run with great passion. The generations will stand together in faith and refuse to compromise. There will now be a bold declaration that Jesus is the Way, the Truth, and the Life, and there is no other way into heaven. This movement will be very focused. It will not be confused; it will not vacillate. It will not hesitate or be silenced. This movement of Holy Spirit will not be intimidated, passive, or bogged down by politically correct language. It will not be double minded or mired in apprehension. It will be a movement that moves in the burning fire of Christ's presence. A movement ablaze with the Gospel of the Kingdom.

Holy Spirit is firing up a remnant that walks in unwavering obedience to Him. We are entering into the greatest time in human history, in which the remnant is about to see God activity as it has never been seen before. The days that we have been praying forth for years have already begun; thus, we must get into step with them. We are not waiting on God; He is waiting on us. When the angel touched Isaiah's lips, the question was, "Who will go for us?" All God is listening for is, "Here am I, God. I'll go." Like the 500 who were instructed to gather in the Upper Room, you have to choose to either participate in God's Kingdom extension on the earth or to miss out on the greatest revival the world has ever seen.

chapter three

ANGELS
MINISTER TO US

Angels on Assignment

The following translations of Hebrews 1:14 explain the role of angels in the lives of God's elect:

Are they not all ministering spirits, sent forth to minister for them who shall be heirs of salvation? (Hebrews 1:14)

Isn't it obvious that all angels are sent to help out those lined up to receive salvation? (Hebrews 1:14 MSG)

Therefore, angels are only servants—spirits sent to care for people who will inherit salvation (Hebrews 1:14 NLT).

Angels are...commissioned to serve the heirs of God's salvation (Hebrews 1:14 PNT).

Are not all angels spirits that serve Him—whom He sends out to render service for the benefit of those who, before long, will inherit salvation? (Hebrews 1:14 WNT)

Never Worship Angels

Angels have been sent to minister to us, but it is very important that we are balanced in our view of angels. We must understand the rules of engagement where angels are concerned. *We must never worship angels.* Angels are created beings; they are not deity. God alone gets all of our worship.

In Revelation 19:10, the apostle John, who was receiving revelation concerning heaven and the marriage supper of the Lamb, fell at the feet of the angel who was releasing the revelation (which is something angels are sent to do). The angel immediately stopped him saying, *"See that you do not do that! I am your fellow servant, and of your brethren who have the testimony of Jesus."* The Amplified Bible reads, *"Refrain! [You must not do that!] I am [only] another servant with you and your brethren who have [accepted and hold] the testimony borne by Jesus. Worship God!"*

Angels are to be honored and respected as fellow servants. Colossians 2:18 warns that the worshiping of angels is condemned and could cause us to be robbed of rewards. Angels are serving spirits. They serve God like we do and we are to consider them our fellow servants assigned by the Godhead to assist us, the heirs of salvation. *We are heirs; angels are not heirs.* Never worship an angel.

The Angel Network

About ten years ago, I began to think about the various networks that are evident in our nation, especially those of apostolic and prophetic nature. There has been a vast effort to organize (network) the apostles and the prophets into this new campaign God wants to do right now. This networking has been going on since the early 1980s. As I was thinking about where I fit in all of it, what my involvement ought to be—what I should be doing—and the various networks in general, the Holy Spirit spoke to me in a way that has now guided me in several directions. He asked me very clearly, *"What about My angel network?"* The Holy Spirit has a way of asking and making a statement at the same time. All of a sudden, I was riveted upon that phrase—*angel network.* I had never before thought of the angels as being networked.

I remember pausing and thinking, "Well yeah, God didn't create millions of angels only to see if He could. He didn't say, 'Let's make some angels and see what they will do. It might be amusing.'" Angels were made and networked for a purpose. They are disciplined into an organized army, dedicated and focused on their assignment, which is Christ's heirs. *We* are the assignment they have been given.

Partnering of Networks

I began to think about the potential of all the networks partnering with the angel network under Holy Spirit supervision and how it has never been done to fullness.

Since the 1950s, the five-fold ministries have been organized into amazing networks. Simultaneously, evangelism networks were established with such figures as Billy Graham, Oral Roberts, and T.L. Osborn.

In the 1960s, pastoral networks and great churches came into being with pastors such as Jack Hayford and Tommy Barnett.

In the 1970s, teaching networks began with Kenneth Hagin, Kenneth Copeland, and others.

In the 1980s, prophetic networks began all over America and around the world with men and women of God like Chuck Pierce, Dr. Peter Wagner, and Cindy Jacobs.

In the 1990s, apostolic networks began. All of these were brought into existence for this season. The Holy Spirit is about to pour fresh fire and blow fresh wind on each of them, giving them an activated, organized angel army network to assist. It is beginning right now!

Ministry to the Heirs of Salvation

Remember that Hebrews 1:14 says that angels are ministering spirits sent forth to minister for those who will be heirs of salvation. "Ministering" is the Greek word *leitourgikos,* which means "to bring release, to be a public servant, or to perform religious or charitable functions" (Strong, G3010). Angels are sent to minister relief and strength to the heirs of salvation.

Heirs (*kleronomeo*) are possessors. They inherit or receive an inheritance (Strong, G2816). The dictionary defines an heir as "one who receives or is entitled to receive something." Jesus paid full price for us to receive salvation. Romans 8:17 says, *"Now if we are children, then we are heirs—heirs of God and co-heirs with Christ"* (NIV). Because we are recipients of God's inheritance, we are entitled to receive *soteria*—salvation.

Soteria is the Greek word for salvation. It means "rescue, safety, healing, deliverance, preserve or preservation" (Strong, G4991). *Soteria* has three main aspects:

- It is employed first for the natural, earthly realm, indicating material and temporal deliverance. Luke 1:69, Acts 7:25, 27:34, Philippians 1:19, and Hebrews 11:7 are references in which we see angels networking to bring temporal or earth-realm deliverances.

- Second, it is used to reference spiritual or eternal deliverance. You can see that in Acts 4, Romans 1, Romans 10, and Ephesians 1:13. Those passages refer to salvation as a spiritual deliverance when spiritual bondages and strongholds are broken.

- Finally, it is used for present, now, real-time salvation. We find this in Philippians 2:12 and 1 Peter 1:9.

To tie these three aspects together, angels minister to the *kleronomeo soteria*, the heirs of salvation, in both the natural and the spiritual realms in our present time. Don't just think future. Some angels are assigned to regions, while others are assigned to churches.

These ministering angels rescue us and provide safety. They preserve and protect us, the heirs of Christ. They minister certain aspects of salvation to us, assisting our deliverance and destiny. They are present-time deliverers. *Now-time deliverers.*

Narcissists No More!

I have often thought about strategies concerning God's Kingdom and how to implement a new campaign for our King in a region. I have pondered the problems of the past that have stopped every move of God throughout history. Most of them were related to the church as an institution or people who allowed Satan to deceive them. What do we do about this? How do we get past the narcissism, the "about me" mentality? How do we get past the pharisaical bondage? I became more and more convinced that we could not get it done without divine assistance. It has been tried all the other ways and not yet been accomplished! If this is going to be a New Testament campaign, there must be supernatural intervention. There must be miracles, signs, and wonders. Without them, this assignment is powerless. No matter how hard we try or how much effort we put into it, it requires divine intervention if it is going to succeed. The true remnant New Testament church's assignment requires divine ability manifesting through it, or strategies to affect our region cannot work.

The Heir Force

One day, I again drove out to the lake to pray and to think about the angel network and the strategies needed to overcome narcissism in the church. As I was pulling alongside the lake, the Holy Spirit spoke another word to me. This word was very forceful and bold. Although very rare for me, He spoke this word audibly and so loudly that I had to pull the car over to the side and stop. I was shaking. The words were like a command as He boldly said, *"Release my Heir force,"* meaning the force behind the heirs. I knew immediately he meant "heir" and not "air." That word became an apostolic assignment that I have since carried everywhere I've gone.

Just as the United States military has an air force that can be called in to rescue its own or called in to deliver blows to the enemy, this "Heir Force" can be sent to deliver a region. The church has an Heir Force organized by the Godhead to help us unlock the regions for this present-time salvation (*soteria*). They are organized to open up the heavens, to scatter and shatter powers of darkness encamped in regions, to thwart the strategies of hell, and to partner with apostolic teams. They are organized to assist, empower, deliver, and rescue. We have an Heir Force behind us empowered by God Himself. With it, we will affect change, bless and release provision, and make the campaign He has ordained successful. *It is time to release this Heir Force.*

Prophetic Confirmations

During this season, Holy Spirit began to confirm His word with amazing prophetic words. It is important to note that I told the prophets nothing about what was happening concerning angels. Prophet Mark Chironna came to speak, and he prophesied this to me: "You will be wooed by My Spirit into the depths of My presence, and you will be awakened into the awareness of angel ministry." Wow, was that happening!

Then Prophet James Goll came to our church and prophesied this: "Angels are being released and a Rex Humbard anointing for communication and miracles will now open." Then he led us in this decree, "We declare that angels of heaven are welcome in this earth realm. You are welcome here, you are welcome in this region, you are welcome in this state where all things are possible to them who believe. We speak this forth. *Angels on assignment, angels on assignment, angels of His presence, angel messengers welcome.* We declare that the angels of God are being released to us and we shall be strengthened by heaven's arsenal. We shall be strengthened, we shall be reinvigorated. We have supernatural strength *as heaven's army is being released in this region.*" What a confirmation.

Then, Prophet Barbara Yoder came and prophesied, "I am delivering the church out of the religious structure that has held it captive. And the Lord said, shout, shout, shout, for I am cutting the ties. Not only am I cutting the ties, but the Lord says I am loosing my angelic hosts. They are moving throughout this entire territory and region. They are taking the words you have decreed and they are beginning to go forth to bring them to pass."

Prophet Jane Hamon came and prophesied this: "The Lord says, 'I want you to know that I have assigned specific angels who are going to work with you and walk with you.' The Lord says, 'I want you to know that I am going to release My big guns to you.' There's going to be times that Michael comes and works with you. There's going to be other times that Gabriel comes and talks to you. 'There's already been some revelation that I released to you that you have not understood,' and the Lord says that the angel Gabriel—just like he came to Daniel and brought understanding of hard things that were too hard for Daniel to understand—the Lord says, 'I am going to send My angel Gabriel, and he is going to bring understanding to you so that you can move forward into this next season.'"

Prophet Chuck Pierce came to do a Destiny Bible School for us and brought with him Ann Tate, who prophesied, "The Lord says that in this season I will send Lord Sabaoth, the Lord of the Angel Armies, suddenly to a gathering. When He arrives you will have a moment to decide if you are going to align with Him or not. As you align with Him, as you make that choice and that decision, you will so agree with the armies of the hosts of God that He is able to amass and to align the armies of the hosts of earth. The Lord says, 'This must come forth because My pulpit was called to compete with and pull down the thrones of iniquity that abode in the territory; My pulpit has not contended with them.' The Lord says that in this season, 'In order to enter the Kingdom battle I am calling you to that will make a difference on the earth, there will have to be a new alignment with Lord Sabaoth, the Lord of the Angel Armies. As you align I will release the angels in new and greater dimensions as you stand in place with Me.' The Lord says, 'I have chosen you for this purpose, and as Ohio aligns the rest of the nation will begin to shift and align with the hosts of the armies of heaven.' The Lord says, 'I care not if it is only the 300 of Gideon, it will be enough.'" Again, what confirmation!

Prophet Chuck Pierce prophesied that we were to build a firewall around the state of Ohio. Jane Hamon followed with this: "Churches will come from all around the region and dip their torch in your fire." In prayer with our apostolic council, we developed the following strategy:

- There are 88 counties in Ohio, and we would go to every county and hold a county-wide prayer assembly, inviting the pastors and intercessors of the county to attend. We would make some 50 prayer decrees over that county declaring awakening and reformation. We would also loose the Heir Force. We have now been to numerous counties all over the state.

- I also had a prayer torch made that we could pass from church to church. The concept is simple—each church prays 24/7 for one week's time and then passes the torch on to the next church. At the time of this writing, over 600 churches have hosted one of our prayer torches, crying out for revival in our state.

- We have also started political action groups to identify those with our DNA who are running for government positions. We are praying for them daily and we certainly are voting for them.

- And we also have started War Eagle nights for the coming generation. Those nights are called "The Cry."

There is not a doubt in my mind that none of this would be possible without Holy Spirit and His angels. The angels have been partnering with this campaign, connecting us to places and people, as well as engaging alongside us in spiritual battle. The enablers from heaven have been working hard to assist the campaign.

King David's Insight on Angels

Psalm 103:19-22 says, "*The Lord hath prepared his throne in the heavens; and his kingdom ruleth over all. Bless the Lord, ye his angels, that excel in strength, that do his commandments, hearkening unto the voice of his word. Bless ye the Lord, all ye his hosts; ye ministers of his, that do his pleasure. Bless the Lord, all his works in all places of his dominion: bless the Lord, O my soul.*" Holy Spirit inspired King David to use incredible wording in this passage. The word *excel* is the Hebrew word *gibbor*. It means "warrior, valiant one, or champion" (Strong, H1368). But *gibbor* is the same as the Hebrew word *gebulah* or *gebul*. That is important to understand because *gebulah* means "territory, region, boundaries, landmarks, coasts, or limits" (Strong, H1367). Angels help maintain boundaries for the Kingdom of God. They are Holy Ghost led border patrol agents. They assist us in maintaining our regions. They are warriors valiantly fighting to open territories or guard territories. They help us set the landmarks that state, "God rules this territory." They help set the landmark that says, "This is Kingdom territory. This is God territory. God rules this geography." When an apostolate declares what God says into their regional (territorial) assignment, angels hearken and help clear the territory and establish the rule of King Jesus. They assist all His works in all places of His dominion. When we declare the dominion of King Jesus over a region, angels begin to assist in establishing it. Fellow servants begin to patrol the boundaries. They will war in the natural realm or the spirit realm. Fellow servants will then begin to administer the covenants we have declared there in Jesus' name.

- *Strength* (Hebrew: *kowach*)—force, to be forceful, to be firm, or to produce. They are hearkening to produce the Word of God that's been decreed (Strong, H3581).

- *Commandments* (Hebrew: *dabar*)—business, cause, matter, or purpose.

- They do the King's business in the region (Strong, H1697).

- *Pleasure* (Hebrew: *ratson*)—desire, will, or inclination (Strong, H7522). They do whatever the King is inclined to do. They do whatever He wants done. They do whatever the other self, Holy Spirit, wants done.

It's easy to see that the angels' assignment and our assignment is very similar. We are also to do whatever the King is inclined to do. We are to do whatever He wants. We are to establish His reign in our territory. We are to establish His will in our region. We are to set boundaries that declare, "God reigns here. Entering Kingdom territory. Entering God territory. Entering territory where the King's covenants are maintained, guarded, and enforced by Holy Spirit, by saints here, and by the angel armies." We are to declare His dominion. We are to declare against hell's forces, "Your strategies are off limits. You cannot enter." If we dare declare the Word of the Lord and prophesy what it says, His hosts will then mobilize. And great victory, deliverance, and miracles can come into our region—*we can shift the territory so it aligns with the Word of God!*

chapter four

THE INTRINSIC NATURE OF ANGELS

In Need of Assistance

Over the past ten years, I have been on an assignment to study angels, so that I may teach the body of Christ. While this does not make me an expert, there are certain aspects of the apostolic angel doctrine that I recognize as happening around us right now. We need to be keenly aware, discerning the times and understanding what we should do (see 1 Chronicles 12:32). To do this, we must understand how the Holy Spirit uses the angel network because that will give us enlightenment, revelation, and guidance.

Again, Hebrews 1:14 states: *"Are they not all ministering spirits, sent forth to minister for them who shall be heirs of salvation?"* Angels are sent to assist the heirs of salvation, those who have received Jesus as their Lord and their Savior. Because God in His wisdom sent the angels to aid us, we must conclude that we need the assistance. We must also conclude that it is His will for us to have that assistance or He would not have sent it.

Dependent Destiny

Our destiny and purpose are God provided and were designed before we were ever born. Scripture clearly points out that our destiny and purpose are interdependent. In other words:

THEY ARE DEPENDENT ON THE HOLY SPIRIT

There are certain aspects of my destiny that I will never achieve without the Holy Spirit. Romans 8:14 says that we must be led by the Spirit to manifest the fact that we are sons and daughters of the living God. I need the power and support of the Holy Spirit or there are aspects of my destiny I will never accomplish.

THEY ARE INTERDEPENDENT UPON OTHERS

In other words, I need your help. There are certain parts of the destiny God has in mind for me that I will never achieve without your help. I need people who will assist and support. We cannot reach our purpose without the help of one another. I need help, I need a push, and I need encouragement. A lot of people have done things they never thought they could do simply because someone else believed they could do it.

There are areas in which others encourage you, and thus you are able to attain a different level in order to get things done—in some cases, things you never thought you could do. You see, it is important that we encourage one another. "I think your potential is off the charts. I don't believe you've even tapped into what you could do!" We need each other to stir up our potential in Christ.

THEY ARE ANGEL ASSISTED

There are some things about my destiny that God in His wisdom decreed the angels would assist. This is New Testament doctrine—God's plan. He sent the angels to assist us. It is His will. Now, with that in mind, the times in which we find ourselves today require us to understand the nature of angel servants and the inherent tendencies that direct their conduct. The work we do together can accelerate and be fulfilled at a different level with their assistance.

Intrinsic Nature of Angels

To fully utilize anyone who becomes your assistant, you must understand his or her personality. How does he think? What has been her life's experience? What is his background? It would help to understand her personality profile and what training she may have had. If you know the person's skill and personality composition, you can partner with that person more productively. Now yes, the assignment of angels can vary, because God commissions them to do all kinds of things, but their intrinsic values and nature are consistent. Let's take a look at the intrinsic nature of angels, so that we can translate it into an understanding relevant for this season.

INTRINSIC VALUE OF ANGELS

Angels are very intelligent and wise. In 2 Samuel 14:20, Joab, through a widow woman, told David he was as wise as an angel and he knew what was happening on earth. Angels know what is happening on earth. The word *wise* in Hebrew is *chakam*, which means "shrewd, prudent, cunning and clever" (Strong, H2450). Our angel assistants are not odd, naïve beings. There are many in the body of Christ today who seem to think, "If it is odd, it is God!" Odd does not mean supernatural. We need to be supernatural in our operation, and if you understand God's nature you will understand that. It is not odd that God could create the world. If you understand who He is, you will think, *Of course He could do that; He's supernatural.* Angels are supernaturally *wise* beings, not *odd* beings.

ANGELS ARE PATIENT BEINGS

Numbers 22 tells the story of a rebellious prophet named Balaam. In some ways, it's one of the funniest stories in Scripture. Balaam wanted to help the Moabites (enemies of God's people), but God sent an angel down to stop him. As Balaam rode along on a donkey on his way to help the Moabite officials, an angel got in the path of the animal. Balaam did not see the angel standing in the path, but the donkey did and bolted off the road. This angered Balaam, and he got down and beat the donkey. Finally, he got the donkey back on the path, but the angel once again blocked the way. When the donkey bolted again, Balaam repeated his beating. This happened three times, until God enabled the donkey to speak. I do not know if God laughs the way we do, but this would have been a good time to do so! The donkey turned around and said, "Why are you beating me?"

Balaam responded, and then God opened his eyes so that he could also see the angel. The angel then said, "Why are you beating the donkey? Surely, if he hadn't stopped, I'd have killed you." What a sobering thought. It was as if the angel said, "You're not going to get to the Moabites, because I am on assignment to stop you!" I want you to see in this account that the angel was patiently carrying out his assignment. Though the time was extended, and at least three attempts were made, the angel patiently did as he was told.

We are assisted by very patient beings, and this patience cannot be compromised. They are committed to their assignments and will faithfully stand to complete them. They do not quit. I am confident some angels have been patiently waiting, in some cases for years and even decades, for the saints to move so that they could also move. They have been waiting for the decrees necessary to go forth to change a region. They have been waiting for a remnant who would be proactive and turn things around. They have been patiently waiting for years for various individuals—maybe even you—to turn around and fire up for God so that they can assist them with their God-given destinies.

ANGELS ARE MEEK BEINGS

Jude 9 says that when Michael the Archangel was contending with the devil about the body of Moses, he dared not bring against him a railing accusation but said, "The Lord rebuke you." *Meekness* does not mean *weakness.* Michael simply used his authority. He used *delegated authority,* which simply means *given authority,* from the Godhead. He did not bother making accusations against the devil. He was there to take care of business, and that business was taking care of the body of Moses, who had passed away.

We are assisted by meek beings who powerfully use their authority in the Lord. They do not flinch when dealing with demons. They do not flinch when dealing with Lucifer and his kingdom hierarchy. Rather, they both carry great authority and wield it. "The Lord rebuke you" is similar to how we say, "The Lord Jesus." In His name, we rebuke the adversary. Kenneth Knox translates it this way: "Michael was content to look at Lucifer and say, 'The Lord rebuke you,' or 'Jesus rebuke you.'" To rebuke means to convict or punish. He was saying, "The Lord punish you; the Lord will convict you, and I will be patient until your punishment comes. You will be locked up forever, and I will be patient until that time." He did not allow himself to become emotionally involved with demons. Never allow yourself to fall into that trap either. Use your authority like Michael did. His assignment was to take care of Moses' body. The assignment of angels today is to take care of Christ's body, which is the church. They will do that without becoming emotionally involved with demons; rather, they will use the authority they carry to protect the body of Christ.

ANGELS ARE JOYFUL BEINGS

Luke 15:10 says that there is joy in the presence of the angels over just one person coming to Christ. Thankfully, we do not have sad angels floating around us as our assistants. No, Christ's Kingdom is righteousness, peace, and joy in the Holy Ghost. It is hard to have an assistant around you who is sad. Angels sing, dance, jump, and shout; they are not mopers, gripers, or whiners. Heaven is a whine-free zone—hallelujah!

ANGELS ARE POWERFUL AND MIGHTY

You can forget those Michelangelo paintings of angels who look like little sissies. God has no sissy angels! Second Thessalonians 1:7 says the Lord will return to the earth with His mighty angels. *Dunamis* is the Greek word meaning "mighty" (Strong, G1411). *Dunamis* might is God's power, capable of anything. It is the power like that released when dynamite is lit and explodes. Angels carry with them the released energy that makes God who He is. They are powerful because they carry His miracle-working power. Don't think of weak, dainty fairies floating around when you consider the angels. Think of powerful, mighty beings of light who come from the presence of King Jesus. They are carriers of His divine energy and glory!

John writes in Revelation 18:1, *"And after these things I saw another angel come down from heaven, having great power; and the earth was lightened with his glory."* John most likely witnessed an archangel. This is one of at least three divine assistants to one of the Persons of the Godhead. This particular angel was Michael, the war angel, who assists Father God. He represents the power of the mightiness of God. Whenever Israel is in battle, Michael is present as God the Father is protecting. When Father God moves in the Scriptures, He moves with Michael as His assistant.

The angel who assists the Holy Spirit is Gabriel, a messenger bearing God's Word, bringing guidance and direction. Gabriel is the angel who visited Mary to inform her and direct her by proclaiming that the Holy Spirit, whom he assists, would come upon her. He also visited both Joseph, to inform him of the news of Jesus' conception, and Zechariah, to inform him of Jesus' arrival. All throughout the Scriptures, we see Gabriel coming with messages from Holy Spirit.

The angel who was the assistant to Jesus Christ was Lucifer. His primary role was worship leader until he rebelled and came against God in heaven. When he rebelled, he fell out of the Throne Room in a flash and landed on earth, where his rebellion continues today. But he was first an assistant to Jesus Christ. That is why God the Father or the Holy Spirit did not come and die for our sins. Why Jesus? Because the Trinity understands authority and alignment, and They will not step outside of that. Jesus said that He delegated authority to that archangel, so He would go to earth and would not return until He got back the authority He delegated. That is why He rose up out of the grave proclaiming, *"All authority (all power of rule) in heaven and on earth has been given to Me"* (Matthew 28:18 AMP). This means that now, in His name, we can use that authority; now we have taken up the position of power that the fallen archangel Lucifer once wielded while assisting Christ. The same works that He does, we do also. We are the assistants; we have Throne Room ministry. And we also have assistants—the angels. It is very important that we understand authority and how it works, making sure that we stay within biblical parameters. We have mighty angel assistants on our side who help us accomplish what we ourselves cannot accomplish alone.

ANGELS ARE OBEDIENT

Psalm 103:20 says, *"Bless the Lord, you His angels, who excel in strength, who do His word, heeding the voice of His word"* (NKJV). The Hebrew word for "heeding" is *shama*, which means "to come to attention like a soldier, to perceive intelligently and obey, and to give undivided attention for the purpose of obeying or fulfilling" (Strong, H8085). Angels stand to attention when the Word of the Lord is declared. They heed it. Sons and daughters speak the voice of God's Word on this earth. When we speak the Scriptures, we are speaking God's Word. When we make decrees, angels snap to attention to bring that Word to pass. They don't hearken to our word; they hearken to and obey the Word of God that we declare.

ANGELS ARE HOLY

Mark 8:38 says, *"For whoever is ashamed of me and of my words in this adulterous and sinful generation, of him will the Son of Man also be ashamed when he comes in the glory of his Father with the holy angels"* (ESV). Jesus called the angels holy. They are morally and ethically pure, uncontaminated by the world. They are ethically obligated to hear the decrees of God's Word and to bring them to pass. If you see something that is unethical, corrupt, or tainted, rest assured the angels will not be involved with it. There is a lot happening in the name of the Kingdom right now that lack ethics and integrity, yet there is a claim that angels are backing these things. Understand this: angels will back nothing that lacks integrity; they will not back anything unethical. What you see in these situations are familiar spirits, counterfeits, demons. We must learn to differentiate! We must be able to recognize what is contaminated, what is a demon or familiar spirit, and what is of God. If we know the difference, we will function as we should.

ANGELS HAVE WILLS

Isaiah 14:13-14 shows us that before his rebellion in heaven, Lucifer is described as a being who had a will. He said, *"I **will** ascend into heaven, I **will** exalt my throne above the stars of God: I **will** sit also upon the mount of the congregation, in the sides of the north: I **will** ascend above the heights of the clouds; I **will** be like the most High."* He and the angels who followed him chose to do so because they could. Of course, they chose wrongly and were judged for it. Angels think and make decisions. The angels who serve the Godhead, and us, serve by choice. In other words, they desire to do this; they are not *made* to. This is an important point, because an assistant who is forced to serve you, rather than choose to, lacks passion or zeal. Our angels serve the saints, Christ's Kingdom, with passion and zeal. We must conclude that they are sold out to this campaign of the Holy Spirit, unwaveringly loyal to Him and how He leads, yielded to the authority figures above them. Because this is so, they carry heaven's authority delegated to them. Because of their obedience, they are now walking in power, sold out to the mission. It is important for us to understand that we have zealous beings right behind us, who have made their choice to push this campaign of the Holy Spirit. When working with the angel network, you are working with wise beings, authority-carrying beings, and powerful beings. They are anointed with *dunamis* power, moving with passion and doing so willingly.

ANGELS HAVE SPIRIT BODIES

Angels have hands, feet, heads, mouths, hair, faces, and voices. This allows them to appear in our three-dimensional realm of length, breadth, and height, looking exactly like us. When their assignment requires it, they can appear in our world or dimension and look just like you and me. Hebrews 13:2 says, *"Be not forgetful to entertain strangers: for thereby some have entertained angels unawares."* Another translation says, *"By doing this, some people have welcomed angels as guests, without even knowing it"* (CEV). The New Living Translation says it this way: *"Don't forget to show hospitality to strangers, for some who have done this have entertained angels without realizing it!"*

The question is, how close would an angel have look like a man in appearance for you to meet one and not know it? They must be extremely close to a man in appearance when they want to be visible in the human realm, and clearly that requires some assistance. First Corinthians 15:44 says, *"There is a natural body, and there is a spiritual body."* Both are real! The natural body is temporary and the spiritual body is eternal. Actually, the Scriptures teach that the spirit body is more real. The Amplified Bible reads, *"[As surely as] there is a physical body, there is also a spiritual body"* (1 Corinthians 15:44 AMP)

The Bible clearly teaches that our heavenly angel network is real. Angels are not phantoms, they are not imaginary, they are not ghosts, they are real! Our assistants are not illusionary. We have real, intelligent, wise, and powerful beings networking together with us in this new Kingdom campaign that is beginning now. We have real help for our assignments!

Angels Need No Rest

Revelation 4:8 states this. I am glad that I do not have a worn-out angel like Clarence in *It's a Wonderful Life*, who has to earn his stars or bars. No, the angels assisting us say, "Go ahead and sleep; I have it covered. You need strength; I already have it."

Angels Work in the Visible and Invisible Realms

Numbers 22 and John 20 speak of this. They work visibly on earth and spiritually behind the scenes. They operate in our natural realm, becoming physically involved if need be.

Angels Eat Food

Genesis 18:8 and 19:3 illustrate this. I think God allowed these accounts to be included because He wants us to know how real heavenly beings are. You must be real if you can eat. The children of Israel ate angel food in the form of manna for forty years. Psalm 78:25 refers to manna as angel food. Angels shared what they had with God's people. No doubt they were involved, bringing it daily.

ANGELS TRAVEL AT INCONCEIVABLE SPEEDS

Revelation 8 and 9 show us that angels can move through the heavens quickly. They move at accelerated speeds on behalf of the people of God and as quick responders. As beings of light, they can get anywhere on earth in the twinkling of an eye. Remember, light speed is 186,000 miles per second!

ANGELS ASCEND INTO HEAVEN AND DESCEND BACK TO EARTH

In Genesis 28:12, Jacob dreamed of a ladder that reached heaven, with angels ascending and descending upon it. He renamed that place Bethel, meaning "House of God," and one spot in particular, *Mahanaim*, meaning "the place where two angel camps protected the coming generation" (Strong, H4266). Clearly, angels were coming and going.

In Matthew 4:11, Jesus was in a fierce battle with Lucifer. At the end of this spiritual warfare, angels came and ministered to Him, probably bringing Him food and water after His forty day fast. Angels had ascended and descended upon the Son of Man. Angels are seen again coming and going.

In John 1, while picking his disciples Jesus met Nathaniel. Nathaniel was surprised by Him saying, "I saw you when you were under the fig tree and Philip told you about Me." Jesus then made this statement: *"You've become a believer simply because I say I saw you one day sitting under the fig tree? You haven't seen anything yet! Before this is over you're going to see heaven open and God's angels descending to the Son of Man and ascending again"* (John 1:50-51 MSG). Jesus was gathering together disciples for a new earthly campaign, something that had never been done before. Nathaniel did indeed see that angels were ascending and descending upon the Son of Man. Clearly, angels would be ascending and descending to assist the disciples on the earth just as the angels had assisted Him in His spiritual battle.

Jesus is beginning another campaign in our times and is calling for apostles to follow Him. Holy Spirit is coming with fresh outpourings and with the angels of Heaven to accomplish God's purpose. Angels are ascending and descending, ministering great strength to the overcomers. The church, empowered by the Holy Spirit, will be a true House of God, a Bethel. A place where angels will ascend and descend. Angels will go into the presence of King Jesus and return with their missions. They are the Lord's Hosts organized to lead Holy Spirit's campaign.

Be a Doer

An angel network is laboring to bring about the decrees of the saints, the bold declarations of Scripture. They circle around Holy Spirit-led worship. By implication, an assistant or a helper helps someone do something. Angels help us do things in the Kingdom, but they do not do our work for us. They are not slaves; they are assistants. In other words, it is expected that *you* do something. Angels do not help those who do nothing. They are not assisting the passive, uninvolved, uncommitted, lackadaisical, or lukewarm Christian. You must be a doer of the Word to tap in to heaven's network. Those doing nothing are often the ones who are complaining that the Kingdom is not working for them. Do something and watch the assistance start. Be a doer, actively engaged in Kingdom advancement locally, regionally, and throughout the world. Be engaged against the powers of hell. Don't just talk about prayer, but be a doer of the Word after praying the Word. If we give our time, talent, and finances, angels will assist us. The two areas in which you will see the most angelic activity are worship and prayer. Worship is a form of song decrees, while prayer is heart decrees to God. The unifying factor here is that we must be people who decree the Word of God to activate angels.

While establishing vision for the future is important, we also want to operate in the now. Great boldness must come upon us, including boldness for signs, wonders, and miracles. The angel network will assist us. They will ascend and descend upon Christ's heirs. It is time for the greatest campaign that has ever been—the Third Great Awakening! Millions of angels are available to assist us with our God-given assignments. We must understand that we need this support of angels. If God the Father needs it in heaven, how much more do we, His sons and daughters, need it on earth?

The alarm clock of heaven is ringing on the nightstand of a sleeping church. It is time for us to rise to the occasion. The question becomes, will you be a doer? When Christ returns, what will you be found doing? The "watchers," or angels, are watching for us *to do* something. Are you doing what God says? Are you a doer of the Word or a forgetful hearer? Many today are forgetful hearers. James 1:22-24 says, *"But be ye doers of the word, and not hearers only, deceiving your own selves. For if any be a hearer of the word, and not a doer, he is like unto a man beholding his natural face in a glass: for he beholdeth himself, and goeth his way, and straightway forgetteth what manner of man he was."* Do not forget who you are. You are a King's son or daughter. You are a person of authority, here to rule and reign in life through Jesus Christ. You are here to be a participant in the King's Third Great Awakening. Do something for the King and the angels will assist you. *The greatest days in church history are not in the past; they are now!*

chapter five

HOW ANGELS ASSIST YOUR DESTINY

Take heed that ye despise not one of these little ones; for I say unto you, That in heaven their angels do always behold the face of my Father which is in heaven (Matthew 18:10).

An amazing benefit of the ministry of angels is how they assist the releasing of destiny. Angels help the heirs of God and joint heirs with Christ to understand their purpose and potential. This is vital to understand. Quite frankly, because of poor teaching, no teaching, or a western mindset that has trivialized angels, millions of believers today just wander through life not understanding the real purpose for their being. We can understand, and angels are sent to help us understand.

The Scripture reveals that to see our destinies come to fullness, we all need assistance. No one achieves great significance in life without a lot of assistance. We need the assistance of the Holy Spirit. He is the number one source for direction and guidance. Also, we need each other. Much of our destiny is interdependent. That's why we need the church and the body of Christ. Without others mentoring, instructing, resourcing, assisting, working with us, some of our purpose will never be accomplished. Also, there are aspects of our destiny that we will never see come to fullness without angel assistance. We need to understand and embrace that God decided that it be that way. God decided that we would need to be angel assisted to accomplish at least some of our purpose. In their wisdom, the Godhead provided "destiny enablers," sending angels to assist the heirs to discover and release their potential.

Born for Such a Time as This

To see the greatest move of God in history, this must happen. I believe it's why Holy Spirit has led the church through a great season of transition. People are being shifted and connected to times that they were actually born for. It's happening everywhere and there's a sense that we are here for such a time as this. I know in many ways, I myself feel that I am now entering into times that were ordained for me before I was ever born. It's as though I have been prepared up until now for days that are about to unfold. God's remnant people, the remnant believers, are beginning to think similar types of thoughts—*I am here for the greatest harvest in all of history, I am here for now, I am here for the great outpourings of the Holy Spirit, I was made for these times*. Acts 17:26 says that God appoints your time and your place. The reason you are here right now is because God wants you here right now. You could have been born 500 years ago or during the Persian Empire, but you were not. God ordained your time and place (geographic location). You're alive now because God wants you alive now. That means there is something in your destiny that the world needs now, especially the area in "the boundaries of your habitation." God in His infinite wisdom knows this, and with

Holy Spirit assistance, angel assistance, and the body of Christ assistance He wants it released.

> *You made all the delicate, inner parts of my body and knit me together in my mother's womb. Thank you for making me so wonderfully complex! Your workmanship is marvelous—how well I know it. You watched me as I was being formed in utter seclusion, as I was woven together in the dark of the womb. You saw me before I was born. Every day of my life was recorded in your book. Every moment was laid out before a single day had passed* (Psalm 139:13-16 NLT).

Before you were ever born, before there was a single day to you, God wrote down plans and destiny He had in mind for you. Before you were ever put into your mother's womb, He recorded in His book things about your life. That's amazing to contemplate. The Godhead actually wrote down things about you. Second Timothy 1:9 says, *"Who hath saved us, and called us with an holy calling, not according to our works, but according to his own purpose and grace, which was given us in Christ Jesus before the world began."* Again, before time began God established your purpose. "Purpose" is the Greek word *prothesis* and it's one of my favorite words to talk about. *Pro* means "before, to set before, to set up beforehand, or an exposition." *Thesis* means "a written report, an essay, or a composition." *Before you were born, God wrote your thesis.* He wrote your purpose and the plans He had for you. There was a day somewhere in the eternities past when the Godhead sat down and contemplated why they would allow you to be. They contemplated why you would come to the earth, why they would make you, and what would be your purpose. In their book they recorded an essay on you. In Jeremiah 29:11 God says, *"'I know the plans I have for you,' says the Lord. 'They are plans for good and not for disaster, to give you a future and a hope'"* (NLT). God has great plans for every one of us. Your future is bright and your destiny is good. There are no disasters planned by God for your life. The enemy may have some planned, but God and His Kingdom do not. His plans are only good and they are designed to give you a bright future filled with hope.

Consider again the text in Matthew 18:10 where Jesus says concerning angels and little ones, children, or infants, *"Take heed that ye despise not one of these little ones; for I say unto you, That in heaven their angels do always behold the face of my Father which is in heaven."* Angels are plural in that verse, so it is at least two. It could be more, but it's at least two. Because there are billions of these guardian-type angels, there would be twelve billion guardian angels for the six billion people. Not to mention all of the millions of other angels who are busy doing the ministry of God or are busy assisting apostles, churches, visions, or the word of the Kingdom.

> *For I tell you that in heaven their angels have constant access to my Father* (Matthew 18:10 TLB).

> *I tell you that in heaven their angels always are in the presence of and look upon the face of My Father Who is in heaven* (Matthew 18:10 AMP).

> *Be careful that you never despise a single one of these little ones— for I tell you that they have angels who see my Father's face continually in Heaven* (Matthew 18:10 PNT).

There is no scripture the Old or New Testament that indicates we ever lose these angels. Christ tells us that they are assigned but never that they are taken away from us. Dr. Kenneth Hagin writes in his book *I Believe in Visions* about a time when Jesus appeared to him with his angel and said the angel had a message for him. Then Jesus described to him how angels are messengers and came to reveal this to us. He ended the appearance to Dr. Hagin by saying, "You do not lose your angels just because you grow up."[1] Indeed, Scripture implies the opposite. The ministry of angels may be limited in your life due to unbelief, disobedience, sin, passivity, lack of understanding, or negative speech. Anything that limits the Godhead limits angels. There has to be unity to see their work, but the Bible consistently teaches the ministry of angels no matter the age.

In light of this great benefit that Jesus Himself points out, the angels assigned to your life are most certainly briefed about your destiny. How could they assist your purpose if they don't understand it? How could they assist your destiny unless they were briefed about what your destiny is? The angels who constantly view the presence of God in heaven are taught by the Author of your purpose what your purpose is, and they are constantly looking for a time, place, or event to loose you into that purpose. This magnificent benefit shows the love, value, and special care the Godhead provides the believers in Jesus. There are no creatures anywhere on earth except the born-again ones who have this kind of care provided. You are highly treasured with divine destiny planned for you. This is emphasized by the fact that angels were assigned to help you accomplish it the day you were born!

Luke 1 (Mary)

Angels briefed and assigned to assist our destiny is revealed throughout the Scriptures. In Luke 1:30, the angel Gabriel knew that Mary was to be the mother of Jesus. It was in her thesis. He knew that was her destiny before she did. Gabriel actually revealed this to her and was there to help bring it to pass. Obviously, he was briefed on her destiny before he ever showed up. His words and actions would not have been possible any other way.

Luke 1 (Zechariah and Elizabeth)

Luke 1 tells us the testimony of the high priest Zechariah and his wife Elizabeth. They were physically unable to have children, but barrenness was not their destiny. The angel Gabriel appeared to Zechariah one day and revealed God's plan for his life. *"But the angel said unto him, Fear not, Zacharias: for thy prayer is heard; and thy wife Elisabeth shall bear thee a son, and thou shalt call his name John"* (Luke 1:13). It was Zechariah and Elizabeth's destiny to have a son, and the angel of the Lord revealed that destiny to them. The angel clearly knew it before they did.

The angel also knew John's destiny although he was not yet born. There was not one cell to John's life yet. It had just been prophesied that he would come into being. Though yet unborn, the angel knew John was to be like Elijah. He was not to drink wine or strong drink, and he would prepare the way for the people of God to come and receive Jesus. The angel knew this because it was in John's *thesis*.

Acts 27

In Acts 27 we read that the apostle Paul was a prisoner on a ship traveling to Italy when a fierce storm arose. It soon became evident that the ship was going to be destroyed. Just before this happened the angel of the Lord appeared to Paul and told him not to be afraid because he must be brought before Caesar. He gave Paul a destiny word. The angel knew it was God's plan for him to go to Rome and appear before Caesar. Because of Paul's prayer and obedience, angels were released to tend to that destiny, conducting a miraculous rescue at sea whereby Paul and everyone on board made it safely to land.

Notice the angel said to him, "You must get to Rome." "Must" is the Greek word *dei* meaning "necessary by the nature of something, obliged, personal obligation, or unavoidable" (Strong, G1163). The angel said, "This is not avoidable. You have to get to Rome." This is a destiny assignment. In Acts 27:24 the angel said, *"Do not be afraid, Paul. You are destined to stand before Caesar"* (NABRE). Don't be afraid—you have a destiny appointment. By the angel revealing himself to Paul, the angel was assuring him, "The angel armies are behind you, and they are going to get you to Rome."

Are there destinations in life that angels help us get to? Absolutely yes. They constantly try to connect you to a time, a place, or an event that will connect you to destiny. They can preserve, deliver, rescue, lead, and guide us to divine appointments and ordained places. Angels understanding our destiny can help us arrive safely at God-scripted destinations. Have you ever been in a situation that turned out to be a great blessing or a great connection for your life and you wonder, *how did that happen?* Perhaps it was not an accident or coincidence; it was destiny and angels connecting you.

Judges 6 (Gideon)

In Judges 6, we read the story of Gideon. He was threshing wheat in the bottom of the wine press for fear of the Midianite armies. Israel's harvest had been stolen from them for seven years as the Midianites raided and plundered their land, food, and flocks, and because of it the people of God were impoverished. In fear, the Israelites ran to the hillside and hid in caves. So Gideon took his wheat to the winepress one day, and while he was threshing, *"there came an angel of the Lord, and sat under an oak which was in Ophrah, that pertained unto Joash the Abiezrite: and his son Gideon threshed wheat by the winepress, to hide it from the Midianites. And the angel of the Lord appeared unto him, and said unto him, The Lord is with thee, thou mighty man of valour"* (Judges 6:11-12). In verse 14, we read that the angel told Gideon to go in the strength he had and rescue Israel from the Midianites. Clearly the angel of the Lord knew Gideon's destiny, his *thesis.* It was God's plan for Gideon to rescue Israel—the angel certainly knew it before Gideon did. He understood Gideon's assignment when Gideon was still fearful. Although he was hiding in fear, the angel knew his potential and addressed it by calling him a mighty man of valor. Gideon, with the spirit of God upon him, accomplished

God's purpose for his life. He and 300 warriors routed the Midianite armies and stopped the plundering of Israel's harvest.

Potential means latent abilities. They are abilities inside of you that you don't know are there. There are some abilities inside of you that you have never thought about. Angels know about those potential abilities and are constantly trying to draw them out by connecting you to a time, an event, or a place that will unlock or loose your potential. Angels who know your destiny and have been briefed on potential God put in your thesis go to work to bring it out of you. *You are potent with destiny that is angel assisted.*

Genesis 24 (Isaac)

When it was time for Isaac, Abraham's son, to take a wife, Genesis 24:7 tells us that an angel knew Rebekah was in his destiny or *thesis.* This was long before Isaac knew anything about it. An angel led Abraham's servant to her though she was in another country. Please note, the angel knew exactly where she was drawing water. He knew the time and place and connected Abraham's servant to the spouse ordained for Isaac.

Genesis 18 (Abraham)

In Genesis 18, three strangers approached Abraham. We know at least two were angels. The other might have been the Captain of the angels Himself, Jesus. Many believe the account was a theophany, an appearance of Christ in the Old Testament as an angel. The angels told Abraham that in about a year they would visit him again and he would have a son. At this point, Sarah was 89 and Abraham was 99, seemingly too old for such a word to be true. Yet when the angels returned, Abraham and Sarah did have a son—Isaac. The angels knew beforehand that it was in Abraham's destiny to have this son of promise and they communicated that message to him, working to bring it to pass. *A miracle birth ensued just as the angels said.*

Genesis 32 (Jacob)

In Genesis 32:24, Jacob wrestled with an angel all night over his destiny. Do angels wrestle with you about your destiny? Absolutely. They are tenacious about it. Jacob had been a liar, a deceiver, and a crook who connived his way through life. He stole his brother Esau's birthright by deceiving his father, Isaac, into thinking he was Esau in order to get the blessing. Because of that Esau was filled with rage. Jacob fled and stayed away from his family for twenty years, fearful that Esau would kill him at first sight. After those twenty years, we are told an angel of the Lord appeared to Jacob in a dream and gave him a message from the Lord. Genesis 31:13 says, *"I am the God of Bethel, where you anointed the pillar and where you made a vow to Me. Now arise, get out of this land, and return to the land of your family"* (NKJV).

With fear and trembling, Jacob decided to obey. He worked for months to prepare his family to make this return to his homeland, although he still feared Esau and what he might do to his family.

In 1988, God began to wrestle with me about my destiny. It was three years of wrestling over the apostolic call on my life. I did not understand apostles at that time. No one had ever really taught me about it. The only thing I knew about apostles were the ones in the Bible. I went through a time when people kept telling me I was an apostle; they would prophesy that to me. It meant nothing, and in fact, I didn't want to be an apostle, I just wanted to be a pastor. So I brushed off anything apostolic. I was in that mindset for three years, but the wrestling didn't go away; in fact, it got more and more intense. I became very dissatisfied with who I was inside. I knew that there was something more the Lord wanted to draw out of me.

Toward the end of this season, I was in Indianapolis to teach a weekend spiritual warfare seminar. On Friday I was in the hotel room by myself and I had taken the day to be alone with the Lord. I was in that room praying, and as I was praying through the morning an amazing event took place. As I lay on the floor, the angel of the Lord came into the room as a large being of light. I was face down for over an hour afraid to move. The presence of the Lord was all over the room and my mind was going every which way wondering, *What is this about, Lord, what do You want to do?* I had become very pliable before the Lord saying, "I will do whatever You want."

The angel of the Lord who now accompanies my life in other ways gave me this message, "The Lord has called you to be an apostle for Him, and you are to begin saying that you are an apostle and do it publicly. Even on TV, anything that you're involved in, you are to say that you're an apostle of the Kingdom of God. In other words, you are to accept the mantle and the office."

Again, I was wrestling with that. "Lord, I don't understand this." At that point I didn't understand that whatever you do as an apostle isn't about you, it's about Him. In myself I have no authority and I can't do anything. It's the office that carries the authority, but I didn't understand that. I was just looking at my own limitations not understanding the authority of the Kingdom given through a mantle.

The next day I was driving home from Indianapolis and I had two hours to talk to the Lord. I finally said to Him, "Holy Spirit, why do I have to do this? Why are You asking me to do this?"

He said so clearly, "Because I cannot do in the region what I want to do until you do." I took that the wrong way and I thought I had been deceived because God can do whatever he wants in this region. He doesn't need me. I was thinking it couldn't be God and it was just something I made up in my mind. I came back and that

Sunday morning I did not get up and say I was accepting the mantle as an apostle in the Kingdom of God. I just got up and preached. The whole time I was speaking I began to see something I had seen five years before. During prayer, I saw a picture of a wagon wheel and spokes of light going everywhere, and God was speaking to me about a regional assignment. While I was speaking, I began seeing all of that in the room no matter where I looked.

Afterward, I grabbed one of our elders and said I needed him to go with me to Georgia so I could bounce some things off a person I thought would understand this. We flew down there the following week, and I told him when I got there about the encounter with the angel in my hotel room. I explained to him that I thought I received a word from the Lord but was doubting it now.

After hearing me out, he said I needed to look at it another way. He told me to go to Matthew 16 where Jesus asked His apostles, "Who do men say that I am?" Peter said, "You're the Christ, the Son of the Living God." Jesus said, "You're blessed. For flesh and blood hasn't revealed this to you. And on this rock I will build My church. The gates of hell will not prevail against it."

I said, "Yes, but I know he is not going to build His church on the apostle Peter."

He said, "No, you missed it again. Who was the apostle Peter?"

"Well, he was an apostle," I replied.

"Yes, on the rock of revelation that is revealed to the apostles He will build His church." It suddenly clicked. I understood there was a mantle coming upon me and there were some things in this region that are going to be have to be bound and loosed. God needed an apostle's mantle to get it done. It isn't about me, hasn't ever been about me, will never be about me. It is the authority of the Kingdom of God.

After accepting this apostolic call, different angels were assigned to my life and I knew it. The angels knew my destiny. They knew it before I did. They knew it while I was wrestling about it. They knew what I could potentially be because it was in my thesis. One of them appeared to me in Indianapolis and said, "Stop wrestling and start decreeing who you are. Accept the mantle. It's not about you." It has changed the way I walk, and my destiny has gone to a different level.

The wrestling you have been going through might be the angel saying, "Stop wasting your potential and become who you're supposed to be." *You have a God-planned future filled with great hope before you.* Like Jacob, and like me, stop wrestling with it and decree it.

NOTE

1. Kenneth E. Hagin, *I Believe in Visions* (Tulsa, OK: Faith Library Publications, 1994), 132.

chapter six

WAR EAGLES
AND ANGELS

Angels with Sashes

I have already mentioned some of the angelic visitations I have experienced—a key one having occurred at Caesar's Creek, when the Lord spoke to me to release the Heir Force, the angel network. Two weeks after hearing those words, I was preparing to walk up to the platform and preach on a Sunday morning when I looked up into the balcony and saw two extremely tall angels. They appeared to be about ten or twelve feet high. The angels wore different colored sashes; one had a beautiful sapphire blue sash and the other had a purple sash. Under the sashes were glistening white robes. This was significant to me because the three previous times I had seen angels, they had appeared as glistening, white light beings. This time there were colors, and although I knew the colors were significant, I did not know the symbolism at that time. Thinking back on it now, it amazes me that this visitation did not startle me or throw me off. It seemed perfectly natural that the angels would be there, almost as if I was expecting to see them. I continued the service without saying anything about what I was seeing, because I did not know what the colors meant.

That week, I began a new study—colors and their prophetic meanings. I had not thought much about color prior to this angel sighting, but I quickly began studying them in earnest. It was a fascinating lesson that I shared with my congregation the following week. I discovered that royal blue refers to God's throne, the heavens, and the high priest's mantle. Blue symbolizes heavenly graces and represents grace in the Scriptures. Primarily though, blue represents the Holy Spirit's presence or ministry. Purple in Scripture represents royalty. Kings wore purple and fine linen (purple and white). Purple represents a king's authority and wealth, but primarily it symbolizes his authority. To be clothed in purple and fine linen means you are clothed and anointed with authority. While praying and fasting, an interpretation of that came to me, and a prophetic word became very clear. The Lord said, *"It is time for a fresh release of My Holy Spirit. Power will be poured out, and the King's anointing and authority will increase in unprecedented, delegated proportions. The angel network is assisting the Holy Spirit in exalting heaven's King. Now the young and the old will participate together in the greatest movement of the Kingdom in history."*

The Trans-Generational Anointing

The anointing poured out will be trans-generational, just as the movement was on the day of Pentecost. I began to have a vision—not of handing the baton to the next generation, but of a rowboat. I saw myself rowing a boat, and behind me were teenagers, rather than those of my generation. The Holy Spirit said, *"It is time to row together."* I believe we are in the season for the generations to begin rowing together under the anointing of the Holy Spirit. It is a *kairos* time, which means a strategic "now" time (Strong, G2540).

It is now time for the generations to "team" together utilizing the gifts, talents, and abilities of each—to present Jesus and His Kingdom to our world. What incredible potential is before us—Holy

Spirit and His angels partnering together with the young, the old, and the in-between can truly disciple nations.

While pondering the meaning of trans-generational anointing, Holy Spirit gave me a prophetic word. It has become part of the apostolic call upon my life to help the coming generation be released in ministry. I was preparing to open my Sunday morning sermon when Holy Spirit stirred me to prophesy about War Eagles. He spoke very boldly, calling the coming generation His "War Eagles."

> The Lord says, if anyone attacks you, don't for a moment suppose that I sent them. If any should attack, nothing will come of it. I create the blacksmith who fires up his forge and makes a weapon designed to kill. I also create the destroyer. No weapon formed against you will prosper, and every tongue which rises up against you in judgment, you shall condemn. This is the heritage of the servants of the Lord and their righteousness is from Me, says the Lord.

> An incredible force is being released on the earth. There's never been a warrior force like it before in history. They are going to be called My "War Eagles." They will make up My eagle force, and that eagle force will partner with My angel force and My remnant warrior champions. There is coming now a generation of young warriors who will partner with the remnant warriors who have been championing the call for years. And they will now be called My "War Eagles." They will ride the waves of My glory. They will ride the currents of My winds. They will ride the out-rayings of My presence, and they will begin to manifest the works of My Kingdom. They will demonstrate My power; they will accomplish My will, My way, and they will ride My tsunami wave ablaze with My glory. Not one kingdom will be able to withstand them. My unique eagle force will startle the world with the

intensity in which they stand for Me. The coming generation of "War Eagles" have been groomed and reserved for hell's siege of the earth, and they will now be loosed. They will not bow to the enemies of their God. They will not pay tribute to enemy kings. They will not listen to the propaganda and insults of hell, and they will not allow Me to be lumped in with other gods which are not gods.

They will wrap themselves to Me and I will fly with them. They will twist their grip around Me, and I will mount up with them. We will soar. We will run. They will run carried by Me at speeds never before seen, and we will leap the barriers. We will leap the walls, and we will catapult into demon blockades and break them asunder. We will shatter the gates of hell. My "War Eagles," both young and remnant veterans, will now rise with Me, says the Lord, and they will scream with hunting aggression and ride Me in the battle. They will battle vicious cruel regimes. They will bring deliverance to tortured captives. They will not surrender in fear though surrounded. Though odds may be against them; it will not rattle them. They will not give up though the facts look gruesome. They will not relent though new weapons of war never tried before come against them. New war tactics will only strengthen their grip upon Me. They will fly with My weight to them. The weight of My presence will be braided unto them, and they will circle, and they will dive at incredible speeds, and they will devastate the sentries of hell.

The adversary's kingdom will now become their prey. My unique eagle force will become terrifying splendor to the kingdom of darkness. They will terrify hell's regime because they ride in My presence. My "War Eagles" who wrap themselves together with Me will soar with supernatural power.

They will ride the wind currents of heaven. They will run and not grow weary. They will walk and not faint. My Spirit will renew them. My presence will re-strengthen them. They will mount up with Me on wings as eagles, and no weapon formed against them will prosper; all who rise against them will fall. This is the heritage of My kids, and their righteousness is of Me, says the Lord.

More about Colors

Colors in Scripture often convey prophetic meaning and symbolism. For example, amber symbolizes the Glory of God. You can see that in Ezekiel 1:4 and 8:2. Black refers to sin, death, and famine and sometimes the midnight hours, as shown in Lamentations 4:8 and Revelation 6:5. Brown is used in reference to sheep (Genesis 30:32-33, 35, 40). Crimson refers figuratively to sin. Crimson linen was used in the temple, as shown in Isaiah 1:18 and 2 Chronicles 2:7. Grey describes the hair of the elderly and aging. Red or scarlet symbolizes the blood of atonement, as shown in Isaiah 1:8, Joshua 2:18, and Leviticus 14:52. White represents purity, light, and righteousness (Revelation 6:2, 7, 9; 19:8). Green refers to vegetation, as shown in Psalm 23:2, 2 Kings 19:26, and Revelation 8:7. There are limited occasions when green can also refer to a corpse.

White, Blue, and Purple

There is a prophetic application regarding three specific colors—white, blue, and purple.

White refers to purity, righteousness, holiness, and light. White robes are given to those of us who die as overcomers in Christ (Revelation 3:5; 6:11). The twenty-four elders seated around God's throne are dressed in white (Revelation 4:4). Jesus Himself, when transfigured, was recounted as wearing clothing white as light and His face shining as the sun (Matthew 17:2). We read in 2 Corinthians 11:14 that Satan disguises himself as an angel of light, which was his created status. He was the morning star, the light bearer, but is now just a fallen angel, as are all the angels who followed him. That does not mean there are no more angels of light in the Kingdom of God. Only one third fell, while two thirds stayed to serve God and His people. There are millions of angels of light—pure, holy beings who carry the presence, anointing, and glory of God upon them.

The color blue symbolizes the Holy Spirit. It refers to the heavens or the sky. Blue also symbolizes God's throne and heavenly grace. Sapphire blue is the color of the high priest's mantle, so blue also represents the ministry of Jesus now released by the Holy Spirit. The Holy Spirit came from "out of the blue" at Pentecost, down from heaven, Christ's throne, to be a present minister to the people of God and a high priest now with us. Heaven's grace was extended by the power of the Holy Spirit through grace gifts, or *charisma*, when He suddenly came (1 Corinthians 12). The Holy Spirit stands in Christ's presence and hears what Christ is saying to the church. He then communicates that message to us. Jesus said in John 14:18, *"I will not leave you as orphans; I will come to you"* (NIV). He does that through the Holy Spirit, His Other Self. The high priestly ministry of Jesus is now with us constantly through the Holy Spirit. He is the Spirit of Truth guiding us individually and corporately.

Exodus 24:9-10 tells us that Moses, Aaron, Nadab, Abihu, and seventy elders went up on Mount Sinai. There they had lunch with God in His "spirit" body. They saw God standing on a pavement of some sort, and His color was sapphire blue. Ezekiel 1:26 tells us that the throne of God itself is sapphire blue. Hebrews 4:16 calls his throne a throne of grace. So again, the color blue in Scripture represents the Holy Spirit, the heavens or the sky, God's throne of grace, and the high priestly ministry of Jesus and the Holy Spirit.

Finally, purple symbolizes royalty and a king's authority or anointing. It refers to the garments of the wealthy or riches themselves. In Luke 16:19, Jesus said the rich man was clothed in purple and fine linen. Purple was the most precious of all ancient dyes. It was made from a shellfish found in the Mediterranean Sea, and it took 250,000 mollusks to make one ounce of the dye, which was very expensive.[1] Only royalty or the very wealthy could wear purple. In Acts 16:14, we see that Lydia funded the apostle Paul's ministry by selling purple garments to the wealthy. The Roman soldiers clothed Christ in purple upon His arrest, according to Mark 15:17. Although the act was carried out in ignorance and mockery, those soldiers had it right prophetically, because He is the King.

Prophetic Understanding

This is an apostolic, prophetic word from the Holy Scriptures—that Holy Spirit is breathing fresh wind on in our times. The season of Joel's great revival in Acts 2 parallels what is now beginning. The angels of light have been released to assist us in wearing the white robes of overcomers. With the Lord's angel armies in support, the overcomers will release God's kingdom into the regions of the earth, overcoming the powers of darkness entrenched there. These light beings (angels) are sent to turn the war in favor of the saints. They will assist in opening earth territories to a new Kingdom movement. The wearing of blue and purple sashes on a background of brilliant white linen speaks in confirmation of what the Spirit of God is saying—we shall overcome!

What Joel prophesied is coming with fresh wind and fire out of heaven. God is coming to His church in new ways and with fresh power. Why? Because we have gone to the sapphire throne of grace, and we keep returning. We have encouraged everyone we know to do the same because heavenly graces have been released upon us via the mighty Holy Spirit. Grace gifts, the gifts of the Holy Spirit, will now be released on new levels with the assistance of angels—the word of wisdom, the word of knowledge, the gift of faith, the gift of workings of miracles, the gift of healing, discerning of spirits, tongues, interpretation of tongues, and prophecy. These gifts will now expand in their meaning, demonstration, and manifestation among us. The world has never seen the gifts of the Spirit as they're about to come forth through heirs in all generations. The high priestly ministry of the Lord framed or activated by our confession is increasing in manifestation and will be demonstrated. It doesn't matter what hell tries in opposition; it doesn't matter what the government tries or atheists or terrorists or media or arts and entertainment. The Kingdom of God will be physically seen!

Dead, passive Christianity cannot change this mandate because God will find a remnant somewhere who will receive it. When He does, He will come out of the blue with a dynamic outpouring. He will set them on fire and endow them with so much power that it is going to shake the region wide open. Hell cannot stop it. Indeed, all flesh is the mission of this heavenly campaign and it will be done. The Holy Spirit, the angelic host, and the church, in partnership with the throne of heaven, all agree with the King's command. It is immutable! It will be done! It will be done!

Bold authority is starting to rise up in the church. We are understanding we are not here to play patty cake with hell. We are here to stop it. Aligned with the King of Kings, Jesus, our job is to evict the Devil and his regime from their strongholds. As sons and daughters of God, heirs of Christ, we have been delegated authority to do exactly that in Jesus' name. Angels are ready to partner with that effort. Can the church bring the enemies of our King to His feet to be His footstool? Yes! The church, assisted by Holy Spirit-supervised angel armies, will bind and twist His enemies into a footrest for Him. The New Testament Church will release and experience great deliverance, freedom, healings, harvest, and prosperity. Jesus said it will be a glorious church prevailing over all the power of hell (Matthew 16:18).

The Mayflower Vision

I once had a vision of an old wooden ship with sails, like the Mayflower. This wooden ship was sitting at dock. There were huge ropes—one rope holding it in the front and one rope holding it in the back. Suddenly, a large angel with a massive, sharp axe appeared and walked down to the dock. He approached the front rope and severed it with one cut. The ship was still tied in the back, but the wind caught it and began to swing it around. At first I thought the boat was going to crash into the dock. Just as it was nearing impact, at just the right time, the angel swung the axe at the back rope and severed it as well. The boat did not crash into the dock, but drifted seaward. A huge sail unfurled as the wind hit it. Suddenly I saw a word on the sail—*oasis*. This is the name of the church I pastor, but I knew it was not only a reference to my church, but the New Testament church as a whole. The lettering was bold and brown (remember that brown is the only color that refers to sheep). Prophetic understanding came with great emphasis:

> The New Testament church is being turned around by Holy Spirit wind and angel assistance. What has tied her to the docks (in waiting passivity) has been severed. Freedom to sail in "God breezes" is now hers to enjoy. Also, within those decrees, the voice of the Lord can be heard sounding out a re-commissioning—"Gather My lost sheep. Set sail for My harvests. Set sail for the lost souls I died for. Leave the dock and sail into harvest time."

NOTES

1. *Nelson's New Illustrated Bible Dictionary* (Nashville, TN: Thomas Nelson Publishers, 1995), 288.

chapter seven

ANGELS HELP
CHANGE REGIONS

*So I will restore to you the years that the swarming locust has eaten,
the crawling locust, the consuming locust, and the chewing locust,
My great army which I sent among you. You shall eat in plenty
and be satisfied, and praise the name of the Lord your God, who
has dealt wondrously with you; and My people shall never be put
to shame. Then you shall know that I am in the midst of Israel:
I am the Lord your God and there is no other. My people shall
never be put to shame* (Joel 2:25-27 NKJV).

*But to which of the angels has He ever said: "Sit at My right
hand, till I make Your enemies Your footstool"? Are they not
all ministering spirits sent forth to minister for those who will
inherit salvation?* (Hebrews 1:13-14 NKJV)

A major benefit of angel assistance is how they help apostles, pastoral leaders, and five-fold ministries shift their regions into divine
alignment. It is time for a major shift in our nation and in the church.
It's time to shift into harvest mode, seeing millions come to Jesus. I

believe it is time to see a revival like Joel prophesied, with new out-pourings of the Holy Spirit that will affect all flesh. One that will shift our young men and women from indifferent, listless living to a generation of purpose and destiny. They will prophesy the Word of the Lord. They will declare the principles of God's Word and move in great power and authority seeing signs, wonders, and miracles that God promised would happen. The strongest prophetic and apostolic generation in all of history is now beginning to emerge on the earth. That means there must come a shifting into prophetic revelation at levels we have not seen before. This will produce demonstrations of the "mightiness" of our God. Visible, tangible, undeniable, and nota-ble miracles will be seen on this planet. There will be wonders in the heavens and the earth.

In 2006, while preparing to release this message on angels helping to shift regions, the Lord gave me this prophetic word:

It is time for a fresh release of My Holy Spirit upon the earth. Power will be poured out and the King's anointing and the King's authority will increase in unprecedented delegated proportions. The angel network is assisting Holy Spirit in exalting heaven's King. And now the young and the old will participate in the greatest move of My Kingdom in all of history.

It was a very clear word that this outpouring is going to be trans-generational. Rather than passing the baton to the coming gen-eration, Holy Spirit said, "No, run *with* the coming generation."

So I will restore to you the years that the swarming locust has eaten, the crawling locust, the consuming locust, and the chewing locust, My great army which I sent among you (Joel 2:25 NKJV).

The prophet Joel, under the inspiration of the Holy Spirit, was talking about harvests. Locusts eat harvest. Jesus, the head of the church, referred to lost humanity who needed salvation as harvest fields. Yes, our harvests have been swarmed by demon locusts that have crawled, chewed, and consumed. But we are now entering a new season and the creeping, crawling, chewing demons that intimidated a passive, cold church are simply not intimidating the Kingdom-minded church of our times. We are not intimidated by demons, hell, or any of its strategies. We are here to rule and reign in Jesus' name and bring the enemies of our King to His feet as a footstool. We are here to demonstrate superior power and authority in His name. The devil and his kingdom are not the superior ones. There are more angels with us than fallen ones he has, and ours are far more powerful. There is now a people who are beginning to understand this and move under a new anointing and power of Holy Spirit. They are beginning to understand that the greater One is indeed in them. First John 4:4 is not given to us in order to feed our egos. It is a fact: "*Greater is he that is in you, than he that is in the world.*"

There is now emerging a remnant church that is beginning to believe for lost harvests to be restored. I don't know how many harvests we have lost in America or the world but it has to be a massive amount. God promised through the prophet, "Joel, your harvests are going to be restored. You're going to praise the Lord your God who is dealing wondrously with you. You will never be put to shame. You're going to receive new outpourings of the Holy Spirit. Your sons and your daughters are going to prophesy. I will show wonders in the heavens and in the earth beneath. And multitudes in the valley of decision are going to call on the name of the Lord your God." God says, "*I am obligating Myself to restore your lost harvest. Trust Me. Be faithful. Say what I say. Decree My words and I will make My word good.*"

The wording of Joel 2 is similar to what God promised Abraham, "*For when God made promise to Abraham, because he could swear by no greater, he sware by himself*" (Hebrews 6:13). A Bible oath is spoken seven times because the number seven represents the number of wholeness or completeness. Understanding this gives us great hope. God says, "All of Me says this. Everything I am says this." God swore an oath of obligation to Abraham, and He swears that He will restore our lost harvest. It's an immutable promise! No mutations!

When God activates His promise, accelerating it to fullness, there is a release of angelic assistance. This has been true throughout history, and we are seeing it today. The fresh outpouring of the Holy Spirit that Joel prophesied will now release angels to help apostles and church leaders shift their regions into alignment with God's Word. These angels will assist in restoring lost harvests, the ingathering of new harvests, and times of great restitution, including lost income. These angels will help apostles release great deliverance into their regions and in breaking demon strongholds. This, of course, will increase the harvest, where millions will receive Jesus as Lord.

Are they not all ministering spirits, sent forth to minister for them who shall be heirs of salvation? (Hebrews 1:14)

Angels assist "sent forth" ministry. That is a reference to apostolic ministry or New Testament Kingdom hub ministry because the word *apostle* means "sent one" (Strong, G652). Apostles are sent on assignment from the Godhead and often a region, state, or nation is a part of that assignment. Angels assist this sent apostolic ministry.

Surely the angels are no more than spirits in the service of God, commissioned to serve the heirs of God's salvation (Hebrews 1:14 PNT).

Angels are commissioned to serve our God-given assignments. The Greek word for *angel* is *aggelos* meaning "a messenger" (Strong, G32). Hebrews 1:14 says they are all ministering spirits. *Ministering* is the Greek word *leitourgikos* meaning "to bring relief, a public servant, to perform religious or charitable functions" (Strong, G3010). *Sent forth* is the Greek word *apostello* meaning "set apart, set at liberty, to send out on a mission, and to send from one place to another for business or employment" (Strong, G649). Angels are assigned to places or regions to help do business. Of course, they can also go from place to place. Also, and importantly, *apostello* is a derivative of *apostolos*, which is the Greek word for *apostle*, pointing toward this vital definition: the work of apostles and the ministry of angels flow together, operating hand in hand (Strong, G652). Apostles and angels are divinely linked and assigned together to places or regions.

Jesus, the head of the church, describes the ministry of angels and the work of apostles as linked together in the book of Revelation. The apostle John receives a message from Jesus, which was a message written to seven churches that are in Asia Minor. Notice, there are seven regions specifically mentioned. Each letter begins with the words, "*Write this letter to the **angel** of the church*" (Revelation 2:1, 8, 12, 18; 3:1,7,14 NLT).

The "sent one" to each church is referred to by Jesus as the *aggelos*. Why? Because both angels and apostles can mean "sent ones to a region with a message." Very interestingly, the Hebrew word for *angel* is *malakh,* which also means "messenger" and refers to an ambassador who represents the one who sends them (Strong, H4397). For an angel or an apostle, that would be Jesus or one of the Godhead. Also, *malakh* means one who is commissioned to perform a purpose for God and ordained to complete a God-given purpose. *Malakh* is translated in the Old Testament as prophet, priest, pastor, teacher, and refers to the work of apostles or the work of the sent ones. So in both the Old Testament and the New Testament the work of apostles (sent ones) and the ministry of angels flow together.

Hebrews 2:2 says that angels give messages to the prophets who can then prophesy that message into a region. Those prophetic words can then become strategies that apostles and pastoral leaders run with. I have used this strategy for years now at The Oasis and in the Awakening Now Prayer Network. Our apostolic council meets to pray over prophetic words we receive and then we develop ways to implement the prophecies into our region. This has helped us shift our state toward great awakening. This has also released angel armies to assist us. Our testimony is clear—angels have assisted us to help change our region. Demon strongholds are being broken. The region once called "The Evangelist Graveyard" is now ripe for revival. Angels sent to partner with the apostolic assignment have helped bring great deliverance. Most certainly, angels have enabled us, under Holy Spirit supervision, to shift a barren region into reformation.

Angels Deliver Apostles

In Acts 5, the angel of the Lord brought great deliverance to the apostles so they could then go do their assignments. We read over this sometimes because we don't pay attention and focus on what was taking place.

> Then the high priest rose up, and all they that were with him, (which is the sect of the Sadducees,) and were filled with indignation, and laid their hands on the apostles, and put them in the common prison. But the angel of the Lord by night opened the prison doors, and brought them forth, and said, Go, stand and speak in the temple to the people all the words of this life (Acts 5:17-20).

The apostles were locked up in a common prison, but an angel came and opened the jail, bringing deliverance. Angels fought to keep apostles free so they could do regional assignments. Assistance was given to the apostles for "temple" or "church" ministry. *Confinement was broken and great liberty to continue was given by angelic assistance.* Clearly the apostolic ministry and the fresh outpouring of Holy Spirit along with angelic assistance is of paramount importance if we are going to see regions change. I believe this is beginning to take place in America. Not in vast numbers, but it's beginning. What's happening is we are shifting from confinement to great liberty to minister. We are shifting into mighty deliverance, and angels are here to assist. There are aspects of our assignment that are not possible without fresh outpourings of the Holy Spirit and the release of His angels. Apostolic ministry is absolutely dependent upon it.

Peter

In Acts 12:7, we are told that the apostle Peter was chained up in prison, but the angel of the Lord came, broke the chains, and opened up the prison. Notice again, an apostle and an angel of the Lord worked together. The apostle Peter, with angelic assistance, moved from confinement to liberty. The strategy of hell has always been to try to put the apostles in confinement and tie them up. Why? Because if they ever get free, then regions will shift. As a result of this angel's deliverance, Peter's assignment to the churches in Asia Minor began to bear much fruit. Great revival began to spread as the regions were affected with the Gospel of Christ.

Paul

In Acts 27, the apostle Paul was a prisoner on a ship headed for Rome. A hurricane hit them and the sailors were terrified and thought they were done for. But Paul stood up and said:

> *And now I urge you to take heart, for there will be no loss of life among you, but only of the ship. For there stood by me this night an angel of the God to whom I belong and whom I serve, saying, "Do not be afraid, Paul; you must be brought before Caesar; and indeed God has granted you all those who sail with you"* (Acts 27:22-24 NKJV).

Amazingly, the angel knew Paul's assignment was to go to Rome. Indeed, they did lose the ship, but no one lost their life. Again, an apostle and an angel were on assignment together to a region. They were in partnership for a Kingdom purpose. The Gospel of the Kingdom was being shifted to another nation, going from "Jews only" to Gentiles just as Jesus had prophesied to Paul when he called him on the Damascus Road saying he would be an apostle to the Gentiles. A divine shift occurred, divine protection was given, and supernatural deliverance came forth.

Jesus

Jesus was also a sent one. In Matthew 1, a great shift was taking place on earth. The shift from old covenant to new covenant, from law to grace, was happening. Jesus was sent by God. His mission was clear and angels were involved. Angels were assigned to Christ's coming as Gabriel came to Mary and told her that she was going to give birth to the Christ child. Angels came to Zechariah and Elizabeth, the wise men, and Joseph. Jesus, a sent one, an apostle of the Kingdom, our greatest leader, was coming to change things, and it is abundantly clear that angels assisted Him. Angels helped the Kingdom of God shift into harvest mode. Jesus addressed this in His earthly ministry in Matthew 13:39, saying that angels would become reapers and assist in reaping the end-time harvest. What is all the shaking about on the earth? It's picturing a massive shift in the spirit realm. It's prophesying a major shift in the Kingdom of Almighty God. It's prophesying a shift into harvest mode just like the King prophesied.

Gideon

In Judges 6, the "angel" of the Lord appeared to Gideon. For seven straight years the Midianites raided the people of God and stole their harvests. They were greatly impoverished because of it, but it was time to stop the raiding and the lost harvests. It was time to shift into gathering harvests, and clearly an angel assisted that assignment. The angel was instrumental in shifting Gideon from a passive, intimidated, and desolate existence into a mighty leader of great valor who, with supernatural help, took 300 men and killed 15,000 Midianite warriors. Gideon, a remnant, and angels brought back the harvest.

This is ordained for our times as well. Angels, guided by Holy Spirit, are available to assist us in moving from passive Christianity into aggressive, culture-changing warriors who go get the harvest. Angels are busy drawing valor out of God's people. Also, angels are assisting Holy Spirit in calling forth great leaders, those who will step forward and stop the raiding. Leaders who will persevere and reap great harvest. Leaders who will face overwhelming odds in the natural realm just because God is on their side. Leaders who will go gather the spoil and bring it back to God's camp. Those who will lead an aggressive charge no matter the odds. Those who will attack hell with a remnant.

Joshua

In Joshua 5, Joshua is preparing to lead the people of God into their promised land. It was time for a culture change, a shift from forty years of wandering around in the wilderness to living in their inheritance. A shift from bondage to great liberty. A shift from being owned to owning. When Joshua comes to Jericho and goes to appraise the situation outside of the walls, he comes face to face with a mighty warrior who had a drawn sword. Joshua asks the angel, "Are you for us or for our adversaries?"

The mighty warrior says, "No, I am captain of the Lord's hosts."

Host is *tsebaah*, meaning "a mass of beings organized for war, a multitude of angelic beings organized for a campaign, and a multitude of angel warriors prepared for military service" (Strong, H6635). Remember, our definition for *campaign* is a series of connected activities to get or to do something. *Campaign* means organized action to obtain a purpose. A multitude of angels were organized by heaven's captain to help the people of God obtain God's promise. A multitude of angel warriors were organized for the campaign of shifting God's people into a new region and helping them be established in that region. They networked with the people of God to change their culture from a culture of slavery to one of freedom. The shift was empowered by Almighty God and His angels.

Pentecost

On the day of Pentecost in Acts 2, a massive shift was taking place. Jesus sent His Other Self, the Holy Spirit, to begin a brand new campaign on the earth. As we saw in Joshua's time, the Holy Spirit was accompanied by angel armies. Holy Spirit and His angels shifted the church to new levels of ministry. *Everything* went to new levels—anointing, giftings, fruitfulness, and authority to govern and reign. Heaven's hosts were assisting Holy Spirit in an outpouring of power. They assisted in shifting the ministry of apostles to new regions. Holy Spirit came with angel armies to assist the apostles in transforming regions with the Gospel of Jesus Christ. History records entire regions were affected as God's power produced signs, wonders, miracles, and great healings as Holy Spirit and angels connected their activities to the apostolic campaign.

Why the increase of angelic activity in recent times? Why the increase of signs and wonders in the heavens? I believe it's a confirming sign that it is time for a new campaign of Holy Spirit. Over the past decade we have heard key after key after key concerning the success of an apostolic campaign, but we have been missing the most basic key to all apostolic movements. *The key to any movement is "movement."* You have to move. You cannot always be on vacation. There are times when you must engage. There are some times when you've got to display the courage of a Gideon and stand up in the culture to make a difference. You can't always run and hide. Sometimes you have to engage and go get something that was stolen from you. It's time for the church to arise and take back what's been stolen from us.

It is time in this moment for the people of God to become engaged. Angels are networking with the church under Holy Spirit supervision and they are striking the enemies of our King and His Kingdom. Angels are bringing coals from the altar of heaven to try and fire up the people of God. Holy Spirit is moving to release power for a new beginning, a new outpouring, and a new season to be fruitful and multiply. He is coming to resurrect and renew a movement, not an institution. We are called to be a part of a movement like the 120 in the upper room who turned our world upside down with a Gospel of the Kingdom.

Movements do not sit or stand around dazed and confused, wondering what is going on and why God isn't taking things back from the Devil for them. They get up and they start to move, knowing that if they move, all of heaven will move with them. It's time for the church to get up and move in the power of the Holy Spirit. It's time to move in signs, wonders, and miracles. It's time to move in the gifts of the Holy Spirit again—words of wisdom, gifts of faith, discerning of spirits, healings, and miracles. The church by definition is to be a movement. It is time for the church of the King to begin to move from complacency to focused Christianity. From intimidation to great valor. From hopelessness to faith and confidence in the living God. To move from the four walls into the streets and the marketplace, into government and the media, into business, education, arts, and entertainment. From selfish, "what's in it for me" Christianity to servants of God doing His will. From consumer Christianity to discipleship.

It is time for a new outpouring of the Holy Spirit and for some fresh fire to come upon the people of God. It's time for the apostles and the apostolates to transform their regions with a Gospel of power. It's time to break from confinement to great liberty. It's time for resources to be restored and multiplied. It's time to stop the raids of hell that steal our harvests. It's time to stop wandering around in the wilderness and cross over into a new region. It's time for the church to rise to a new level of power and authority that God has ordained for our times. It's time for God's people on earth to get in sync with heaven and run with the coming generation. It's time for the church to hear fresh orders from heaven and campaign together, releasing the anointing of King Jesus. It is time, in Jesus' name, to shatter the teeth of chewing, crawling, and consuming locusts and, under the breaker anointing of our King, arise to scatter and shatter the constraints of hell, the restraints of government, society, or anything else that gets in the way of the Kingdom of Almighty God. Under Holy Spirit supervision and angelic assistance, *it's time to shift from harvest lost to ingathering!*

chapter eight

BATTLING FOR THE
THRONE OF A REGION

For unto us a child is born, unto us a son is given: and the government shall be upon his shoulder: and his name shall be called Wonderful, Counsellor, The mighty God, The everlasting Father, The Prince of Peace. Of the increase of his government and peace there shall be no end, upon the throne of David, and upon his kingdom, to order it, and to establish it with judgment and with justice from henceforth even for ever. The zeal of the Lord of hosts [angel armies] *will perform this* (Isaiah 9:6-7).

And I say also unto thee, That thou art Peter, and upon this rock I will build my church; and the gates of hell shall not prevail against it. And I will give unto thee the keys of the kingdom of heaven: and whatsoever thou shalt bind on earth shall be bound in heaven: and whatsoever thou shalt loose on earth shall be loosed in heaven (Matthew 16:18-19).

The word *government* is the Hebrew word *misrah*, meaning empire or dynasty (Strong, H4951). Jesus wants His church representing His throne and extending His empire into the territories of their region. *Throne* is the Hebrew word *kicceh*, and it means "the seat of power; seat of authority; canopy under which rule extends; jurisdiction of a position of honor, and the position from which a king reigns" (Strong, H3678). Jesus sits upon the throne of His Kingdom to order it, establishing judgment and justice. He wants His church aligning with Him to accomplish that rule.

Isaiah 9:7 says, *"The zeal of the Lord of hosts will perform this."* The zeal of Lord Sabaoth, the Lord of angel armies, will perform this. Angel armies will partner with and assist the church in battling for the "throne" and in establishing Christ's Kingdom in their region. Jesus will release His armies to assist the church, who obeys His commands, in binding or loosing some things on earth. This is clearly seen in Christ's name for the church, the Greek word *ekklesia*. It is used 113 times in the New Testament, and it is a political word, not a religious word (Strong, G1577). You would think that Jesus would use a religious word, such as *temple* or *synagogue*, but He doesn't. By calling His church *ekklesia*, He uses a word describing the act of governing. Colin Brown, in the *International Dictionary of New Testament Theology*, describes the definition of *ekklesia* as used in Christ's day. It's vital to understand:

> The ekklesia was an assembly of competent citizens of a region who met at regular intervals to govern. This was done by a verbal yes or no or an upraised hand. Their sphere of influence included:
>
> A. Decisions on suggested laws and final decisions on any new laws
>
> B. Appointments to official positions

C. Both internal and external policies in the region including contracts, treaties, war and peace, and financial matters

D. The Ekklesia would rule on cases of treason

E. It could summon for its army to assemble for war

F. The Ekklesia ruled on societal and cultural matters for its geographical location or territory

G. The Ekklesia chose by upraised hands who would sit at the Areopagus, the high court of Athens (similar to our Supreme Court).[1]

Jesus says, *"My church, consisting of My heirs, are to rule and reign with Me in their region."* That is a profound definition and one that is quite different than what you see happening in our world today. In fact, we have many institutions that say they are a church but they stand for secular values, whatever the society says. That is not a proper church. Authority has been given to Christ's heirs, the born-again ones, to make rulings on the earth for or against something. "Be verbal," the King says. We have been given authority in Jesus' name to overrule things on the earth. We can overrule hell's government. We can even overrule natural government by asking for divine assistance. We can ask for angel armies to be loosed to back up the rulings that we make.

While we must be involved in the natural realm by being politically involved, we must also understand that much of what the *ekklesia* battles is spiritual in nature. We are to do spiritual battle with hell's kingdom for the throne of our region, and that battle is intensifying right now.

Notice again that Jesus says, *"Whatsoever thou shalt bind on earth shall be bound in heaven: and whatsoever thou shalt loose on earth shall be loosed in heaven"* (Matthew 16:19). The word *bind* and the word *loose* are both courtroom terms—they are legal rulings. You can have a binding contract or you could go to court and have a contract dissolved or loosed. The Greek text has fascinated me for years. Jesus literally says, in Matthew 16:18-19, when you put all of the Greek tenses to it: "Whatever you at any time encounter of hell's council (hell's leadership/government), that I am determined my *ekklesia* will prevail against, you will then face a decision as to whether or not you will bind it. What transpires is conditional upon your response. If you do purposely and consciously involve yourself in binding the issue on earth, you will find at that future moment when you do, it is already bound in heaven." *Jesus says that what is bound or loosed is conditional upon the church's response.* "If it's bound by My people in My name, or loosed on earth by My people in My name, heaven will back it up. My throne will rule in your favor and sufficient force will be released to enforce it. My angel armies will be sent to assist."

Isaiah prophesies that the zeal of the Lord of hosts (angel armies) will perform this. *Perform* is the Hebrew word *asah* meaning "to work, to procure something, to accomplish, to construct, and to build." *Asah* is also translated in Judges 11:36 as "to make war" (Strong, H6213). Angel armies will make war with hell's kingdom, on the church's behalf, to enforce its "bindings" or its "loosing" decrees. Angels help procure regions. They help us build a kingdom "hub" or "stronghold" according to the decrees that are made by heirs of the region in Jesus' name. The angel armies of Lord Sabaoth will be "loosed" to help the church increase Christ's Kingdom's influence throughout the region.

Angels will also assist us in cleansing the heaven over our region of principalities and powers of darkness (demon princes) of hell's government. Demon princes can be bound and displaced from their iniquitous thrones over a region. They can be removed from a throne and cast down. Their legal rights—because of sin or broken covenants, idolatry, or generational covenant-breaking—can be broken by an *ekklesia* overruling them in Jesus' name and then taking that seat of authority themselves. The battle is for the throne of the region. If you overthrow hell's kingdom in Jesus' name by binding spirit princes and then occupying the seat of power as a vigilant ruling body under Christ's authority, then it's much easier to get rulings accomplished upon the earth because you removed hell's power that was trying to come against it. The battle is won in the spirit before you ever see it in the earth. Jesus said, "If My church will battle for the throne of their region and will bind hell's kingdom, hell's kingdom will not prevail because I, Lord Sabaoth, will release angel armies to enforce their rulings."

I will put together my church, a church so expansive with energy that not even the gates of hell will be able to keep it out. And that's not all. You will have complete and free access to God's kingdom, keys to open any and every door: no more barriers between heaven and earth, earth and heaven. A yes on earth is yes in heaven. A no on earth is no in heaven (Matthew 16:19 MSG).

And I will give you the keys of the Kingdom of Heaven. Whatever you forbid on earth will be forbidden in heaven, and whatever you permit on earth will be permitted in heaven (Matthew 16:19 NLT).

I will build My church, and the gates of Hades (the powers of the infernal region) shall not overpower it [or be strong to its detriment or hold out against it]. I will give you the keys of the kingdom of heaven; and whatever you bind (declare to be improper and unlawful) on earth must be what is already bound in heaven; and whatever you loose (declare lawful) on earth must be what is already loosed in heaven (Matthew 16:18-19 AMP).

The ramifications of these verses are incredible. We are to bind what heaven wants bound and loose what heaven wants loosed by aligning ourselves with the Word of God. Clearly, Christ Jesus expects His *ekklesia* to declare or make rulings in His name. It is to decide what is proper or improper for a region. It is to decide what is unlawful in a region. It is to decide and declare the way culture ought to be. It is important to remind ourselves that Jesus said this, not a disciple, not some other character in the Bible. The King Himself said this. The church is to decree God's Word in a region. It is to declare, "Your Kingdom come, Your will be done in this region, just like it is in heaven."

The church is to rise and sit with Christ in heavenly places or heavenly spheres. A throne, a position of power, is involved. That is what Paul teaches in the book of Colossians:

> *Giving thanks unto the Father, which hath made us meet to be partakers of the inheritance of the saints in light: who hath delivered us from the power of darkness, and hath translated us into the kingdom of his dear Son: in whom we have redemption through his blood, even the forgiveness of sins: who is the image of the invisible God, the firstborn of every creature: for by him were all things created, that are in heaven, and that are in earth, visible and invisible, whether they be thrones, or dominions, or principalities, or powers: all things were created by him, and for him: and he is before all things, and by him all things consist. And he is the head of the body, the church: who is the beginning, the firstborn from the dead; that in all things he might have the preeminence* (Colossians 1:12-18).

Preeminence simply means the ultimate position of authority.[2] Thrones (plural) are created by God, whether visible or invisible. *Throne* is the Greek word *thronos,* which means "a stately seat of authority" (Strong, G2362). Of course, you see that in kings on the earth today. You see their government because it's visible. They rule their territory (nation) from that seat. The same is true of *dominions*, which is the Greek word *kuriotes* meaning "governing power, lord, lordship, and one who possesses dominion" (Strong, G2963).

Principalities is the Greek word *arche* meaning "a leader, a ruler, an originator, or the active cause or causer of something" (Strong, G746). *Arche* can also refer to angels or demons in Scripture. *Powers* is the Greek word *exousia,* and it means "executive power, one with permission to use authority" (Strong, G1849).

All these are visibly seen in the nations governing their regions on the earth today. Of course, to capture a region or a territory, it's vital to capture the throne. You aren't going to get anywhere until you capture the throne. *But what about the invisible?* What about the heavenly sphere? Notice, it clearly says that some thrones and some powers are *not* visible. That doesn't mean they aren't real; it means we can't see them with the natural eyes. God made thrones visible and invisible, and He Himself sits upon the throne of heaven. You cannot see it with your natural eyes but it is a real throne and decisions that are made from that throne affect things upon the earth. Jesus sits at the right hand of God on a throne in heaven.[3] When that throne makes a decree, it affects earth. So don't think "imaginary," think "real but unseen."

The Battle for God's Throne

Before man was created, there was a battle in heaven, where Lucifer and his angels fought for the throne of God. A real throne was fought for, though we cannot see it. This battle is described in Isaiah:

> *How art thou fallen from heaven, O Lucifer, son of the morning! how art thou cut down to the ground, which didst weaken the nations! For thou hast said in thine heart, I will ascend into heaven, I will exalt my throne above the stars of God: I will sit also upon the mount of the congregation, in the sides of the north: I will ascend above the heights of the clouds; I will be like the most High. Yet thou shalt be brought down to hell, to the sides of the pit. They that see thee shall narrowly look upon thee, and*

consider thee, saying, Is this the man that made the earth to tremble, that did shake kingdoms (Isaiah 14:12-16).

The book of Revelation tells us that Michael and his angel army fought against Lucifer and his angels in defense of the throne. Lucifer, of course, was unsuccessful to say the least and was thrown like lightning out of heaven. If Lucifer would dare attempt to take God's throne, why wouldn't we understand that he will attempt to take other thrones?

This is happening in the real, not imaginary, spirit realm right now. Lucifer's idea has always been to occupy the throne of a territory. He wants his kingdom, his fallen angels, his demons to occupy the throne over a region. Why? To affect the natural throne of that region (its government) so that through the natural throne, he can battle against Christ with his diabolical schemes. Lucifer wants his principalities, his powers, his dominions influencing the people of the earth. He wants them working through the natural people, the natural powers, and the natural governments on the earth, so he can empower those who agree with his ideology, his oppressive nature and lust for power. He wants his kingdom empowering and promoting his agenda (like abortion and homosexual marriages) through natural government under demon influence.

Demonic thrones have this assignment: to hinder, confuse, slander, and accuse those who stand for Christ. As with Adam and Eve in the Garden, Lucifer wants his kingdom presenting ideas or thoughts that are not what God says. Why? So that he can usurp the believer's authority and oppress the territory (oppress the Garden).

Ezekiel 28 talks about this. It says that the Prince of Tyrus was a man who ruled the natural earth territory of Tyrus. But it says the King of Tyrus was not a man; it was Lucifer himself. In other words, from the territory over Tyrus (the regional throne over Tyrus) Lucifer controlled the Prince of Tyrus down on the earth. Through the natural government on the earth, the people of Tyrus were oppressed. Similar battles have raged century after century now. Hell's kingdom has consistently fought the church over the throne of their region or nation. It is happening all over America right now. It is happening all over the world, and it is time for the church to realize it and do what Christ said His church should do—bind, tie up, and cast down hell's princes. The church is to use her authority so there's nothing between earth and heaven in their region. It is to also "loose" angel armies in heaven onto the earth to assist her just like God did when His throne was attacked. He loosed Michael and His angels to fight and to defend His throne and they won. The church can loose angel armies and win!

> *War broke out in Heaven. Michael and his Angels fought the Dragon. The Dragon and his Angels fought back, but were no match for Michael. They were cleared out of Heaven, not a sign of them left. The great Dragon—ancient Serpent, the one called Devil and Satan, the one who led the whole earth astray— thrown out, and all his Angels thrown out with him, thrown down to earth* (Revelation 12:7-9 MSG).

It is time for Christ's church to follow His lead and cast out hell's dominions and powers. It's time to displace hell's kingdom princes and, with our decrees of God's Word, loose angel armies who can battle alongside us and cleanse the heavens over our region. It is an assignment that the Lord of hosts says to perform. King Jesus decrees, "Angels, make war alongside of My heirs and expand My Kingdom, cleanse the heavens over them so that nothing interferes between earth and heaven." Obviously, this cleansing of the heavens must happen if we're going to fulfill Christ's command to disciple nations, as Matthew 28:19 says we should do.

Shaking the Heavens Is Promised

A massive shaking of spirit realms over regions is promised in the last days. Hebrews 12:26 tells us that the Lord will shake not only the earth, but also the heavens. We certainly are seeing great shaking on the earth today. Creation is indeed groaning with natural disasters occurring everywhere. Hurricanes, tsunamis, drought, and famines are killing millions of people. Wars, rumors of wars, earthquakes increasing in number and intensity, financial calamities abounding, and great economies are going bankrupt. What Jesus said would occur at the end of the age is being seen in our newspaper headlines.

> *You will hear of wars and rumors of wars. See that you are not troubled; for all these things must come to pass, but the end is not yet. For nation will rise against nation, and kingdom against kingdom. And there will be famines, pestilences, and earthquakes in various places. All these are the beginning of sorrows* (Matthew 24:6-8 NKJV).

> *Whose voice then shook the earth; but now He has promised, saying, "Yet once more I shake not only the earth, but also heaven." Now this, "Yet once more," indicates the removal of those things that are being shaken, as of things that are made, that the things which cannot be shaken may remain. Therefore, since we are receiving a kingdom which cannot be shaken, let us have grace, by which we may serve God acceptably with reverence and godly fear. For our God is a consuming fire* (Hebrews 12:26-29 NKJV).

Shaking the Earth Is Promised

The shaking of the earth has been much talked about in recent times. Yes, thankfully, we are a part of a Kingdom that cannot be shaken. But

He also says that He will shake the heavens. He is not talking about His heaven (the heaven where God lives) that Paul called the third heaven—it doesn't need to be shaken. It's perfect. The heaven mentioned here is referring to spiritual realms also known as heavenly places in the New Testament. The apostle Paul in the book of Ephesians emphasizes this. Ephesians 1:3 says, *"Blessed be the God and Father of our Lord Jesus Christ, who has blessed us with every spiritual blessing in the heavenly places in Christ"* (NASB). The Amplified Bible says in that verse, *"every spiritual (given by the Holy Spirit) blessing in the heavenly realm."*

This includes power and authority in heavenly places, because power from on high has been poured out upon the people of God, upon the church.

Ephesians 2:6 describes what Christ has done for us this way, *"And hath raised us up together, and made us sit together in heavenly places in Christ Jesus."* A seat of governing power is involved. The Amplified Bible reads, *"And He raised us up together with Him and made us sit down together [giving us joint seating with Him] in the heavenly sphere [by virtue of our being] in Christ Jesus (the Messiah, the Anointed One)."* In the heavenly spheres, the church, the *ekklesia*, is to sit down together with Christ on the throne of that region and rule and reign with Him, releasing the power of the Holy Spirit and loosing angel armies to assist in clearing out the demon strongholds that are over them.

Ephesians 3:10, *"To the intent that now unto the principalities and powers in heavenly places might be known by the church the manifold wisdom of God."* The church is to decree the laws, judgments, plans, purposes, and principles of God's Word *to* principalities and powers in the heavenly places. The church, not hell's kingdom, is to define the message and culture of a region. King Jesus commanded that. And if demons get in the way, He says to cast them down and ask for angel armies. The *ekklesia* is to occupy the throne of their region and give an uncompromised Gospel, insisting that the will of God be done in that region and battle with hell to see that it stays that way. If the church will rise up and rule in His name, angel armies will fight alongside of them against hell's power.

Authority to Release Angel Armies Is Necessary

Remember, one of the duties of the *ekklesia* in Jesus' day was to summon and release armies. They had authority to release the army of the region should war be necessary. It is time for the church to pray and summon angel armies to help them cleanse the heavens over them. Ephesians 6:12, *"For we wrestle not against flesh and blood, but against principalities, against powers, against the rulers of the darkness of this world, against spiritual wickedness in high places."* The "spiritual hosts of wickedness" is a reference to fallen angel armies; that is, the angels that sided with Lucifer to attack and try to overthrow God's throne. While they could not do that, they do now attempt to occupy the thrones over regions to pollute earth's territory. There can be no doubt that Christ expects His church to come against them and bind them. The apostle says to wrestle, fight, engage, go to combat with them. We are to put on our armor, as the rest of Ephesians 6 describes, and battle for the throne of the region and disciple it.

We are living in times when Christ's new campaign (that is now being released) is going to shake the heavens. This must happen because God's Word said it will. God is going to shake the heaven. Holy Spirit will empower the New Testament church to topple powers of darkness that are in the heavenly spheres. This word was confirmed by Jesus when He taught His disciples the signs of the end of the age. He finished that teaching by saying the powers of the heavens will be shaken. Heavenly spheres are going to be shaken. Then the Son of Man will appear in the clouds of glory (Matthew 24:29-30). Jesus promised that demon principalities, powers, mights, and dominions will be shaken down from their position of influence by a glorious church. He promised that the authorities of hell would not prevail against His church. We will see a church that confronts these demon princes and demonic strongholds that hinder the coming forth of the Kingdom of God. There is going to be an aggressive church that is going to rise up and say, "No, nothing between me and God. Nothing between earth and heaven."

Dealing with Rebel Kings

Jesus, the apostle Paul, and the writer of the book of Hebrews were quoting the prophet Isaiah about the end-time days, "*Earth is smashed to pieces, earth is ripped to shreds, earth is wobbling out of control, earth staggers like a drunk, sways like a shack in a high wind. Its piled-up sins are too much for it. It collapses and won't get up again. That's when God will call on the carpet rebel powers in the skies and rebel kings on earth*" (Isaiah 24:19-21 MSG). The King James Version says, "*And it shall come to pass in that day, that the Lord shall punish the host of the high ones that are on high, and the kings of the earth upon the earth*" (Isaiah 24:21). Obviously, He isn't going to punish His hosts, His angel armies. But He is going to punish the hosts of darkness (demon armies), as well as "rebel" kings or authorities on the earth. The last great shaking is going to affect both the natural and the spiritual realms. A Kingdom that cannot be shaken is going to shake up and shake down hell's rule in the heavens. It's going to open up the heavens for the rule of Christ's Kingdom. Also, the church that understands her authority is going to take her seat in heavenly places and govern for King Jesus by the decrees she makes. They are going to verbalize a "yes" or a "no" to laws and cultural values within their regions.

Holy Spirit is synergizing the generations together with a fresh anointing of power. He is adding to it angel armies. The battle for the throne of regions is going to be won by the heirs of God and the joint heirs with Christ who have ears to hear what the Spirit of God is saying. We are living at the end of an age with awesome promise. We are not here to be a weak, emaciated, silent body. We are not here to be governed by hell. We are here to dominate hell with superior authority. Awesome days are opening up before us.

The prophetic word from the Scriptures is very bold. The church is to rise and sit with Christ in heavenly places. It is to overrule and overthrow demon powers in a region and occupy the spiritual throne to such a degree that it affects the function of the earthly government beneath it. Christ wants His preeminence in all regions. The church (the *ekklesia*) is to rule and reign with Christ. We are here to occupy the throne of a territory and declare God's way.

The *ekklesia* is to rule and reign with Christ in the spiritual realms over a region and in the natural realms. It's both. Visible or invisible doesn't matter. Natural thrones or spiritual thrones—doesn't matter. Natural dominion or spiritual dominion, it doesn't matter. Natural power or spiritual power—doesn't matter. Why? So that in the visible or the invisible regions, Christ has the preeminence. We are being challenged to step forward and accept an assignment that the church has neglected for decades. It is time to hear the call of King Jesus: *I will have a people who will rise to sit with Me in seats of authority. They will displace demon princes and refuse to allow them to reign any longer.*

Shaking the Heavens and the Earth

In the last days, God is going to shake the heavens and the earth. Lord Sabaoth, Lord of Angel Armies, is going to release angel armies to assist the church in occupying the throne of their region. Angels have been sent to assist the New Testament church in displacing demon princes that are entrenched over earth territories. They help us cast down hell's kingdom leaders. In other words, rebel governments on the earth that oppose God's ways. Rebel government that fights against what God says and comes against the people of God to oppress them. Christ calls to His church (*ekklesia*) to confront and overcome this in His name. He did not put His heirs on this earth to be oppressed by anti-Christ, natural governments. The church is to be a spiritual governing body that overrules natural government oppression. We have not seen it this way and most never teach this, but it's the point of an *ekklesia*. When we refuse to be silent and we stand up for what God says, His superior Kingdom then comes and backs it up. We can rest in confident hope that because of our Kingdom's superior power and superior angel forces, it only takes a remnant to get this done. We must understand that we don't have to have a majority. A thousand can put ten thousand to flight. Greater is He who is in us than he who is in the world.

We are living in the times, prophetically, when Christ is going to empower His remnant to confront and to overrule rebel government with authority that Jesus delegates that is superior. Yes, rebel government is coming against Christ's New Testament church. It is coming against those who are living as best they can according to God's Word. Rebel government through various means (the media, ungodly laws, humanistic values, education that preaches Christians are intolerant losers, and host of other ways) is now attempting to oppress the people of God and the New Testament church. Anti-Christian government is now telling the church what it is to believe, in some cases replacing Christ's own teaching. Rebel government is now forcing its way into the church's doctrine with politically correct compromise—and even worse, doctrines of devils. Sadly, some of our nation's nominal churches have accepted these diabolical changes to Scripture. This is causing great confusion and a watered down Gospel that's powerless.

It is truly amazing that the so-called tolerant ones will not tolerate our beliefs. It is now said with regularity that, "Evangelical Christians need to come on into the 21st century." *Tolerance* to rebels means,

"Believe what we believe. We know what is best. Do it our way or we will attack you in the name of tolerance. You will accept abortion and you will pay for it. We will tax you, and if you don't obey then we will fine you. You will embrace Islam and various other religions as equal to yours. Stop your narrow-minded Christianity. You will embrace a secular agenda. And if you're a Christian and you own a business, we will tell you how to operate that business. You will accept our values or we will bankrupt you. We will put you out of business. We will tell you how to raise your children. We will teach them what they need to know. *We* will teach them their 'core values.' You Christians, just stay out of it."

It's even more amazing that many so-called Christians and some denominations have succumbed to the demon propaganda. In some cases today, the church has conformed to the world rather than conformed to the image and Word of Jesus Christ. America's pulpits, pastors, priests, churches (denominational or nondenominational), and Christians in far too many cases have an unbalanced and unbiblical silence where cultural values (laws, government, leaders) are concerned. We have not made our leaders accountable to truth, so truth is discarded for the convenient ways or the self-promoting ways. We have allowed human reasoning to displace truth. We have allowed experimental philosophies to displace thousands of years of proven sound wisdom. Why? Because the church has refused to be an *ekklesia*. A body responsible for good government on the earth that aligns with the Word of God. And now because we have refused to occupy, to take the seat of the throne of our region, our liberties are being suppressed right before our eyes. Our religious freedoms are being challenged. Our rights are being rewritten or unenforced. And now from coast to coast we see that America is oppressed by rebel, anti-God's-ways government.

Rise Up

Clearly the people of God need to rise up for such a time as this. It is time to cry out against the cowardice revealed by silence.

In Revelation 21, there are eight kinds of people groups listed that are destined for the lake of fire (hell). Liars, murderers, unbelievers, sex traffickers, sorcerers, idolaters, and fornicators. I think it's time for the church to pay close attention to the first one that is on the list—the cowards.

> *But the cowardly, unbelieving, abominable, murderers, sexually immoral, sorcerers, idolaters, and all liars shall have their part in the lake which burns with fire and brimstone, which is the second death* (Revelation 21:8 NKJV).

> *But as for the cowards and the ignoble and the contemptible and the cravenly lacking in courage and the cowardly submissive, and as for the unbelieving and faithless, and as for the depraved and defiled with abominations, and as for murderers and the lewd and adulterous and the practicers of magic arts and the idolaters (those who give supreme devotion to anyone or anything other than God) and all liars (those who knowingly convey untruth by word or deed)—[all of these shall have] their part in the lake that blazes with fire and brimstone* (Revelation 21:8 AMP).

God hates cowards. He didn't put His church here to be cowardly submissive. It's demon doctrine. Franklin Graham, chairman of the Billy Graham Association and also chairman of Samaritan's Purse, when addressing pastors in Washington, D.C. at the Watchman on the Wall National Conference in May 2014, addressed this cowardice.

"The definition of a coward: a coward will not confront an issue that needs to be confronted due to fear. That is a coward," said Graham. "God hates cowards. And the cowards that the Lord is referring to are the men and women who know the truth but refuse to speak it." In his remarks at the dinner session, Graham spoke about the need for churches to speak out against abortion and homosexuality, declaring that "you're not going to shut me up." "We have a responsibility to speak on the moral issues. Abortion, homosexuality, these are moral issues. This is a free country, you can do what you want to do but I want you to know it's a sin against God. This is a sin," said Graham. Graham mentioned how he has "friends who are pastors" who say they want to preach the Gospel and not "become targets." "Well don't you think the Lord Jesus Christ was a target?" asked Graham. "Could we get our heads chopped off? We could, maybe one day. So what? Chop it off!"[4]

Thank God for a bold man who declares the truth!

We Must Speak Truth

There are those today who refuse to speak the truth because they know they will be targeted by those who despise righteousness—Hollywood elites, the media, liberal universities, maybe even the IRS—so they peach a soft Gospel. Their definition of right and wrong is blurred by a politically correct Gospel that sanitizes the truth to the degree that it becomes ambiguous. It's unclear. It's up to your private interpretation. It's whatever you think. It's up to whatever you believe conveniently forgetting you can believe a lie. Millions have and millions do, and millions are damning themselves because they believe a lie. What man believes has absolutely nothing to do with truth; it only determines what is done with truth. Truth means what is absolutely true. You have to go to God to get what is absolutely true. He is truth. Jesus is the way, the truth, and the life. Truth is embodied in His Word, His ways, and His laws, and it's time to stand up for the truth disdaining any "cowardly submissiveness" within the body of Christ.

It is vital we speak the truth without compromise, remembering Psalm 103:20—angel armies hearken to God's Word that we decree. When angels hear us declare what God says they get involved in bringing it to pass. They assist us based on the Word of God. If we want angel armies fighting alongside of us, which we absolutely need if we are going to change nations, then we must declare what God says. If we want the Holy Spirit releasing power from heaven, we have got to agree with the Word of God and speak it boldly. There can be no cowardly silence in the pulpit or the pew. Overcomers speak up and release Holy Spirit power and Angel Armies that affect change in rebel governments.

In the early 1800s, what most today think were the "good ole days" in our nation, we find a different reality. Our government then was corrupt and divided. Slave issues and poverty were stifling our people. The education system was inept. Society was about as bad as it gets. We actually had politicians shooting one another in duels. The church at the time was in passive mode, just like now. The Chief Justice of the Supreme Court at the time was John Marshall, and he wrote a letter to then President James Madison regarding the condition of the church. He wrote, "The church is too far gone to ever be redeemed." Obviously that proved not to be true. It wasn't true then and it's not true now. John Marshall's surmising did not happen because the people of God began to pray. Cottage prayer meetings began to spread from coast to coast. Mid-week prayer meetings began to be everywhere all over the United States. Even lunch hour prayer meetings started. Passionate preaching began to flame from the pulpits and great evangelists came on the scene and began to preach fiery messages of repentance. God's Word was welcomed in the pulpits and proclaimed with holy boldness, and the church was awakened from slumber by the Holy Spirit. It was simply called the Second Great Awakening, and it's going to happen again. There's going to be a third one!

The third and greatest awakening has now begun, and angels from their spheres are going to assist it. It doesn't matter how many chariots the enemy has, their size, or how many demon armies are behind them. It doesn't matter what their philosophies are or how much media they have behind them. They are not a match for the Kingdom of Almighty God. The Lord says, "I will pour out My Spirit upon all flesh," which can only mean that it's going to happen. The remnant church will declare what God says, and angels orbiting are going to hear and they are going to begin fighting alongside of us from their spheres. They are going to fight hell with the people of God and we are going to win. Millions and millions are going to be saved and confess Jesus as Lord. Our King Jesus is going to have His harvest, and hell is not going to stop it.

Indeed, the greatest days in church history are not in our past, they are in our present and our future.

NOTES

1. Colin Brown, *New International Dictionary of New Testament Theology Vol. 1 A-F* (Grand Rapids, Michigan: Zondervan Publishing House, 1975), 291.

2. *Webster's Ninth New Collegiate Dictionary* (Springfield, MA: Merriam-Webster's Inc. Publishers, 1984), s.v. "preeminence."

3. Francis Frangipane, *The Days of His Presence* (Lake Mary, FL: Charisma House, 2012), 52.

4. Michael Gryboski, "Franklin Graham Calls on Pastors," *Christian Post*, May 23, 2014, http://www.christianpost.com/news/franklin-graham-calls-on-pastors-to-speak-out-on-abortion-homosexuality-says-god-hates-cowards-120265/.

chapter nine

WHAT ATTENDING ANGELS DO

But to which of the angels said he at any time, Sit on my right hand, until I make thine enemies thy footstool? (Hebrews 1:13)

Are not the angels all attending spirits sent forth to serve for the sake of those who are going to be unceasing possessors of salvation? (Hebrews 1:14 WIL)

The angel of the Lord encampeth round about them that fear him, and delivereth them. O taste and see that the Lord is good: blessed is the man that trusteth in him (Psalm 34:7-8).

King Jesus is on a new campaign upon the earth. An outpouring has begun—a Third Great Awakening—and according to Holy Spirit, it's going to be very similar to what occurred in Acts 2. Holy Spirit is coming with His angels who will partner with the remnant warriors and with the War Eagle generation (the coming generation) to implement this new move of King Jesus.

In 2006, when Holy Spirit began to download this revelation of angels, He stopped me in my tracks when He made this statement: *"This time I am coming with far more of the angel armies."* That got my attention. He also said, *"The greatest days in church history are not in your past, they are in the future."* I believe that with every fiber of my being. I know something big is breaking on the earth. A movement of God's Kingdom greater than any to date will be seen!

Hebrews 1:14 says angels are *"attending spirits"* (WIL). An *attendant* is someone who attends to another to perform a service to them. A worker in a restaurant is said to tend tables. They wait on the needs of those who are seated at the table. Angels are attendants with tasks that the Godhead has assigned to them. They wait on us, the heirs of God and joint-heirs with Christ. They serve the heirs of salvation.

Angels and Deliverance

Angels protect and deliver those who are committed to Christ and His cause—those who are not compromising His Word and have received Jesus as their Lord. Psalm 34:7 says, *"The Angel of the Lord encampeth round about them that fear him, and delivereth them."* The word *fear* in this verse does not mean scared; it means respect. Angels protect those who respect God's ways, His Word, His church, and His presence. The Living Bible says, *"For the Angel of the Lord guards and rescues all who reverence him."*

Angel is the Hebrew word *malakh* meaning a messenger or one who carries a message. *Malakh* is also the Hebrew word used to describe a prophet or an apostle because all three of them (prophet, apostle, and angel) are *sent ones* with a message. *Malakh* means an ambassador representing the one who sent them. In the angel's case that would be the Godhead. The Father, Son, and Holy Spirit all use angels to accomplish ministry they have ordained. *Malakh* also means one commissioned to perform a purpose for God. The Godhead uses angels to work their purpose. If the Godhead uses angels to perform aspects of their ministry, it should not be surprising that Christ's heirs would also need angels to accomplish aspects of their ministries.

Encampeth is the Hebrew word *chanah* and it means "to pitch a tent, to abide, to set a siege, or to watch" (Strong, H2583). *Chanah* is closely compared to the Hebrew word *chanan,* which makes it even more meaningful. *Chanan* means "to favor, have mercy, show mercy, and it sometimes means to make lovely" (Strong, H2604).

Round about is the Hebrew word *cebiybah* meaning "to circle, to revolve around, or to border" (Strong, H5439). It references protecting our borders (what comes in or cannot come in). The prophet Daniel tells us that the "watchers" are the angels. What an amazing promise this is! Angels, representing Christ Jesus, are commissioned to watchfully circle us and protect our borders. They hover over our lives similar to how they hovered over the 120 in the Upper Room in Acts 2:3. Guarding us, protecting us from demon intrusion, circling us to surround with God's grace. They hover over the heirs of Christ to minister mercy and show kindness. Angels are commissioned by the Godhead to watch over us and make things lovely. (King David says they pitch a tent to do this; in those days they lived in tents). Angels abide, they live, they stick with us, circling us to turn the ugly to lovely.

Most certainly, not everything that happens to us is lovely. You don't have to make things lovely if they are already lovely. Sometimes you need "turn-a-rounders" who make the ugly lovely. Our planet is corrupted by sin. Our culture is polluted by sin. We have water and resources that are polluted by all kinds of things. We have an adversary named Lucifer, and his kingdom is constantly attempting to rob, steal, kill, and destroy us. However, we have commissioned real beings who stick with the assignment of making things lovely. A part of their job description is to take the ugly and make it lovely. Angels surround us with supernatural favor to turn things around.

Ministering Turnaround

We are in a great season in the body of Christ. This is a season for dramatic turnaround in the church, our individual lives, our finances, and, I believe, in this nation. This doesn't mean that everything that happens to us is going to be lovely, but it does mean that everything can be turned that way. Angels are extensions of the Holy Spirit to our lives individually and to our corporate life as a church. They are helpers on assignment to guard the saints.

> *Likewise the Spirit also helpeth our infirmities: for we know not what we should pray for as we ought: but the Spirit itself maketh intercession for us with groanings which cannot be uttered. ...And we know that all things work together for good to them that love God, to them who are the called according to his purpose* (Romans 8:26, 28).

Again, the ugly can be turned around. Miraculous outcomes are in season!

One of the greatest examples of the ugly being turned to lovely occurred on the Day of Pentecost (Acts 2). On that day Jesus sat down at the right hand of Father God in heaven. It was coronation day—the day Jesus was anointed as King of Kings and Lord of Lords. Father poured the horn of holy anointing oil over Jesus' head, which flowed down and dripped onto His body which was seated in the upper room (this is pictured in Psalm 133). What an amazing outpouring! The same anointing on the Head is now on the Body. Amazingly, just fifty days prior Jesus had been crucified. Without question that event was ugly. The cross was an ugly mess. Could that ever be turned around? The heirs know the answer. It was not possible for death to hold Him. Fifty days later, Holy Spirit and His army came into an upper room where 120 disheartened disciples gathered and turned the ugly to lovely!

The word *helpeth* is the Greek word *sunantilambanomai*. It's a phrase that means "to take hold together with" (Strong, G4878). The Holy Spirit and His angels *take hold together with*. Angels circle the saints to get hold of things with them. I know they have gotten hold of things in my own life. Angels are assigned to grab on to ugly situations that we are grappling with and turn them around for good. It's a part of their job description. They are hovering over believers today, attending their lives, waiting for them to declare their freedom and exercise their authority. They are waiting for them to decree what God says in His Word. Angels watch and listen so they can turn things around according to our decrees.

A remnant is beginning to understand that we have an angel army assisting us. Mighty angels with strength, skill, wisdom, and power are available to partner with us in releasing the Kingdom of Almighty God on the earth in greater measure than ever before. The world has never seen anything like it. Hell has never experienced anything like it. In many ways the church has never done anything like it before. New things are on the horizon, things that will startle the world. Christ's Kingdom is going to flow in authority and power with signs, wonders, and miracles exponentially seen!

Even though we face difficult times and situations that turn ugly, *sunantilambanomai*, Holy Spirit, and our angel network can get hold of it together with us and turn the ugly to lovely. Understanding this sets our faith and anchors our souls. While the angels may not be able to bring things full circle to be the same as they were (some things are never going to be the same as they were because of relationship changes, covenant breaking, or even death), and while it may be different than what you wanted or expected, angels assisting Holy Spirit can turn things around for you. *You are never sentenced to a problem if you are an heir. It is a season—not a sentence!* Trust God, declare what He says, and angels will start turning things around!

We are told in Daniel that Lucifer and his angels seek to change times, laws, or seasons. If bad angels do that, how much more can the good angels, anointed by God, change your season? Seasons change. Seasons can come to an end and angels are here to help change and shift the season. I can testify that angels have changed the season many times for me. It's a part of their job description.

Angel Protection

Psalm 34:7 says, *"The angel of the Lord encampeth roundabout them...and delivereth them."* *Deliver* is the Hebrew word *chalats,* and it means "to rescue, to draw out a victory, or to bring forth a victory" (Strong, H2502). *Chalats* also means "to strip away." Angels strip away bonds (spiritual and natural). The apostle Peter was in a real prison, but the angel still set him free. Angels can draw us out of what is hindering us in order to help us win.

When I was ten years old my dad was pastoring a church in Middletown, Ohio. The people across the street attended the church and owned a motor scooter that they would let me ride. I remember one time when I got on it and turned the throttle wide open—a dumb thing for a ten-year-old boy to do. I was flying down the side street when a car backed out right in front of me! I locked up the brakes and began to skid along, and the next thing I knew I was on the other side of that car. It was incredible. I had no idea how it happened.

About that time my dad came walking into the neighborhood, which he never did. He would drive through sometimes, but this time he was on foot and he was looking for me. He said, "A half hour or so ago, I was in the study at the church and I was burdened all of a sudden to pray for you. I began to pray, 'God whatever is happening, protect Tim.'" He was so moved by it that he had to try and find me. I told him what had happened and we went over to where it took place. The skid marks on the scooter went about twenty feet and then there was a blank space of ten feet and then the skid marks went on. I don't know what happened. I don't know if the angels parted the car or picked me up and set me on the other side. All I know is that Satan was trying to kill me because I was doing something stupid, but God heard the prayers of a Pentecostal pastor saying, "Protect my son," and the angels went to work. They protected and delivered.

In 1976, before I went to Bible school, our church participated in a building program in Guatemala. Several of us, including my brother Dutch, went to Guatemala to build a Bible school out in the Petén Jungle. We landed in Guatemala and spent the night in an orphanage. The next day we were to fly out over the jungle, get in a dug-out canoe, and float down to where we were going to build the school. When we went to the airport the morning after staying in the orphanage, the officials at the airline began to argue and tell us they were not going to take us. They said the plane wasn't big enough to carry all of us and our supplies. It looked like we were stuck. Dutch, two other guys, and I got up in a flatbed truck where we could see what was taking place across the fence at the airport and somebody suggested that we pray Psalm 34. So we joined hands and started to pray, "Lord, we don't speak the language, we have no way to get this done, but would You send the angels and somehow break this loose for us so that we can get on our way?" Ten minutes later they came running over and said they would take us, but they wouldn't take our luggage because the plane wasn't big enough. So off we went without our luggage!

That night a great earthquake took place and 27,000 people were killed in the Guatemala City area. By the time it happened we were out in a tent in the jungle. I remember the tent shaking and wondering who was messing with us, but later we began to hear about the massive destruction. After we built the school we went back to the city to help dig people out. We couldn't stay at the orphanage because the two-foot thick, two-story high building had been leveled. I have pictures of where those walls fell across the beds we had slept in the first night. We would have been killed if the angels had not assisted us in getting out of town. I was reminded of Daniel in the lion's den. King Darius came the next morning and said, "Was your God able to deliver you, Daniel?" Daniel 6:21-22 shows us his response, "*O king, live for ever. My God hath sent his angel, and hath shut the lions' mouths, that they have not hurt me.*" Angels had done the same for us. They circled us to protect and deliver.

Angels Lead Us

Another job angels have been given is to lead sinners to those who will witness Christ to them. In Acts 10, we find a fascinating chapter on angels and evangelism. It was time for the apostles to shift their vision to include everyone on the earth. It was time for a different campaign. Christ had given the command for the Gospel to be preached to Gentiles. A new move of the Kingdom was called for, so Holy Spirit and His angels went to work.

An angel was sent to Cornelius, the captain of an Italian band of soldiers, who told him, "Send men to Joppa. Find a man named Simon Peter. Ask him to come visit you and he will describe how you and your household can be saved." Cornelius didn't know Peter, but he obeyed what the angel said.

Meanwhile, the Holy Spirit was dealing with the apostle Peter, saying, "Peter, three men are seeking you. They are Gentiles, but I want you to go with them and don't doubt anything."

At first, Peter argued about it saying, "We can't do that; that's against the law, and that's not how we do things."

But the Holy Spirit said, "It's how we do them now. We are changing things. It's a new day. Christ's sacrifice on Calvary is for the Gentiles also." This, without a doubt, was world-changing revelation being given to the apostle Peter. Holy Spirit said, "It is time for a new campaign of the church on earth. It's time to shift into a different mode. It's time for a new movement. It's time for My remnant to move and embrace a Gentile harvest for King Jesus." That changed everything. It changed the world and history. Holy Spirit supervised it, using angels to make this evangelism shift. Holy Spirit talked to the apostles and sent an angel to talk to Cornelius. Cornelius and his household were the first Gentiles to ever receive and embrace salvation.

When we pray for the lost (an unsaved friend or loved one), when we declare words of freedom over their lives for salvation, angels can assist and begin to deal with them behind the scenes. Peter didn't know an angel was dealing with Cornelius. They were removing the spiritual blinders from a Gentile household. Angels partner with the saints to extend the Gospel message. It's one of the greatest benefits we have. Holy Spirit convicts of sin and the angels lead the lost to those who will witness to them. We need to be willing to pray, "Holy Spirit, I submit to Your ways. Release the angels to connect me to those who need me to witness the power of the Gospel to them."

Angel Appearances and Dreams

This is how Jesus the Messiah was born. His mother, Mary, was engaged to be married to Joseph. But before the marriage took place, while she was still a virgin, she became pregnant through the power of the Holy Spirit. Joseph, her fiancé, was a good man and did not want to disgrace her publicly, so he decided to break the engagement quietly. As he considered this, an angel of the Lord appeared to him in a dream. "Joseph, son of David," the angel said, "do not be afraid to take Mary as your wife. For the child within her was conceived by the Holy Spirit. And she will have a son, and you are to name him Jesus, for he will save his people from their sins." All of this occurred to fulfill the Lord's message through his prophet: "Look! The virgin will conceive a child! She will give birth to a son, and they will call him Immanuel, which means 'God is with us.'" When Joseph woke up, he did as the angel of the Lord commanded and took Mary as his wife (Matthew 1:18-24 NLT).

After the wise men were gone, an angel of the Lord appeared to Joseph in a dream. "Get up! Flee to Egypt with the child and his mother," the angel said. "Stay there until I tell you to return, because Herod is going to search for the child to kill him." That night Joseph left for Egypt with the child and Mary, his mother, and they stayed there until Herod's death. This fulfilled what the Lord had spoken through the prophet: "I called my Son out of Egypt" (Matthew 2:13-15 NLT).

Angels can speak to us in dreams. The angel was very emphatic in these verses, and there's urgency in the warning given by the angel. He said to Joseph, "This baby is about to be killed by Herod. You have to get up and go. You've got to go now, get out of here. Get to Egypt." The angel was clearly instructing Joseph in a dream.

In 1975, I received insight for healings and miracles through an angel in a dream. I believe today that it was an angel assigned to me because of my apostolic calling. Years ago, when I accepted the apostolic calling for my life different angels were assigned to me, and I often hear those angels in healing services telling me of people with a particular sickness or disease that I'm to minister to. It's not unusual for someone in the service to tell me later that they saw the angel standing beside me.

In the dream in 1975, I saw a lady carrying a sack of groceries in both arms and she was saying, "My back is killing me, my back is killing me," as she walked along.

I heard the angel in the dream say, "Release healing to her." I saw myself putting her in a chair and I noticed that she had one leg shorter than the other. I knew her back was out of alignment and causing one leg to appear shorter than the other. I saw myself praying for her and seeing her back and legs adjusted.

The next day Carol and I went to visit her aunt. She wasn't home yet so we were sitting in the living room waiting for her. When her aunt walked in she was carrying two sacks of groceries. She didn't say "hi" or "how are you doing," she said, "My back's killing me."

I said, "Yes and you have one leg shorter than the other and God is going to heal you."

I then did what I had seen in the dream. I asked her to sit in a chair and, sure enough, her legs were different lengths. I prayed and the anointing of the Lord began to adjust her back. It was the first time this had ever happened. It's happened thousands of times now. People fly in from other states sometimes just to have me pray for their backs. She got up and said, "It doesn't hurt, it doesn't hurt!" Then she said, "My neighbor's having back surgery this week, will you pray for him?" So she ran next door and got her neighbor. He came over, smoking a cigarette, and I didn't know what to do except to say, "Get in that chair." He did, and God adjusted his back, and he said, "It doesn't hurt, it doesn't hurt." He was healed, no longer needing surgery. Through the angel's message in that dream, doors of the supernatural have opened time and time again over the years. I know it's a sign and a wonder that I am to release and it all goes back to the angel's instruction in a dream.

Angels Provide Direction

With Cornelius, a Gentile, the angels directed a sinner to someone who would tell him of Jesus, but a believer in Christ can also be directed to a sinner. In Acts 8:26, Phillip was told by an angel to go down to Gaza. He was led to the treasurer of Queen Candace of Ethiopia, who was riding along in his chariot, reading the book of

Isaiah. Amazingly, an angel saw an opportunity to get the Gospel into another nation. No one saw the treasurer doing this, except an angel. A "watcher," as the prophet Daniel refers to some angels, saw what was happening and told Phillip about it. Phillip goes, and upon seeing the man, explains the Gospel of Jesus to him. The man was saved and baptized. The campaign would expand to another nation because an angel led a believer to an unbeliever who was seeking truth!

The New Testament church in our times must shift into evangelism mode as never before. The angels are present to assist us. They are here to connect us to those who are open to the Gospel. The "watching" angels see what we can't see. They see opportunities! We must embrace this supernatural partnership, asking Holy Spirit to release it in full measure. Angels, evangelists, and evangelism must be loosed on the earth by the prayers and decrees of the church. The time is now!

Answers to Prayers

One way that God answers the prayers of His people is through angels. In Daniel 9:21-13 and 10:12-13, the angel Gabriel was sent with an answer to Daniel's prayers. God assigns angels to bring prayers to pass in the lives of heirs. What an incredible benefit. I personally think that is why prayer is fought so much in our churches today. Prayer activates angels more than any other time. Angels attend the prayer time because they are going to get assignments they can begin to work on.

Daniel was fasting and praying for 21 days in Daniel 9 and 10. He needed an answer from God. On the first day, God sent the answer through Gabriel. But we are told that the spirit Prince of Persia, a demon prince, began to withstand the answer and fight it in the heavens. Remember, there are three heavens—the atmospheric heaven, the astrological heavens, and the third heaven, which is God's heaven. God sends an answer, but somewhere in the astrological heavens the spirit Prince over Persia starts to fight Gabriel to stop the answer from getting through. The warfare was so intense it lasted for 21 days. Daniel, with persistent faith, kept interceding. On the 21st day, God commissioned the angel Michael, sometimes referred to as the Prince of Israel, to go down and break up the demon resistance. Michael went with his angels and prevailed against the Prince of Persia's forces, allowing the answer to get through to Daniel.

The answer was available the first day, but spiritual warfare and intercession prayer took place for 21 days. Over and over again through the Scriptures you will see where that kind of prayer causes angels to be released to begin to bring answers. They organize around the prayers of the saints to bring them to pass, especially prayers over nations, regions, and territories. There are many things over a nation or a territory that are not going to be changed unless the angels are "loosed" to assist. That "loosing" authority is given to believers in Jesus' name! Matthew 16:19 says, *"Whatever you forbid on earth will be what is forbidden in Heaven and whatever you permit on earth will be what is permitted in Heaven"* (PNT).

In Acts 12:7-10, the apostle Peter was in prison because of his stand for Christ, but prayer was made by the saints without ceasing for his release. The church held a prayer meeting at John Mark's mother's house. Evidently the prayer and intercession for Peter's deliverance went well into the night. Amazingly, as they were praying for his release, an angel was sent to the jail. The angel released Peter from the shackles, opened the prison door, led him out into the city, opened the gates of the city for him, and brought him to where the prayer meeting was taking place. An angel became an answer to the church's prayer; they cried out for Peter's deliverance and angels were loosed to bring it to pass.

In Genesis 18, Abraham's intercession released angels to bring answers. God came to Abraham and said, "I am going to destroy Sodom because of its perversion." But God, knowing that Abraham's nephew Lot and his family lived there, gave Abraham a chance to intercede for their lives.

Abraham responded with one of the strongest prayers of intercession in all of Scripture. He said, "God, You won't destroy the righteous with the wicked will You? I know You won't do that. If there's fifty righteous in the city, please spare it."

And God said, "If there's fifty righteous, I will not destroy it."

Abraham said, "What about forty-five?"

And God said, "No, if I find forty-five, I will not destroy it."

Abraham kept pleading with God until it was down to just ten. He said, "God if there's just ten righteous in the city, will You destroy it?"

And God said, "No, I will spare it for the sake of ten." Genesis 19:1 says that immediately after Abraham's prayer, two angels were sent to Sodom. These angels led Lot and his family to safety before the city was destroyed. Angels provided escape from judgment for Abraham's extended family because Abraham prayed and angels responded to intercession.

Revelation 8:3 describes how an angel collects the prayers of God's people and puts them into golden bowls. The angel mixes incense (a symbol of praise) with those prayers and then adds in red hot coals from heaven's altar. This causes a sweet-smelling smoke, filled with the prayers of the saints, to rise out of the angel's hand before God's throne. What does God do? He grants what have been the prayers of the saints and releases answers to come forth on the earth! The point of what the apostle John said takes place in heaven is clear. Angels minister, they assist, they help cause to happen what we are praying about. God uses angels to help our prayers be answered.

In the book of Ezekiel, an amazing protection is given to those who pray. Angels are involved in this protection. Throughout the opening chapters of the book of Ezekiel, God talks to him about how the people are involved in abominations. God says detestable things are being done in the nation. He said His teachings are being defied, His decrees are being ignored, His laws are even being mocked.

> *You have been more rebellious toward My guidance and decrees than any other nation, choosing not to live even under the ethical and moral standards of other nations, and certainly not under My laws. ...You have degraded My holy sanctuary with all your detestable images and shocking actions. ...The consequence—violence—has grown up into a rod to punish the wicked* (Ezekiel 5:7, 11; 7:11 *The Voice*).

God promises that a nation that rejects His ways will suffer the consequences. A rod of punishment is released. It will become judgment at some point. Ezekiel 8:6 says, *"Son of man, do you see what they are doing right in front of the temple? The people of Israel are committing shocking actions that drive Me away from My own sanctuary"* (*The Voice*). Sadly this is happening far too much in our times. Abominations, detestable teachings, perversion, heresy, and the ignoring of God's laws by a nominal church are driving Him away from His own sanctuary. Holy Spirit is not welcome in some sanctuaries.

In Ezekiel 9, a remnant who prays and who cry against the abominations is recognized. Special protection from judgment by the angels is given to those who intercede. In Ezekiel 9:4, God said to an angel who was carrying a writing kit and a horn that was filled with ink, *"Go through the midst of the city, through the midst of Jerusalem, and put a mark on the foreheads of the men who sigh and cry over all the abominations that are done within it*" (NKJV). Notice, "put a mark on the foreheads" of the intercessors. Mark those who cry out; mark those who pray; mark those who are crying out against the abominations and are not silent. He then says to the angel, "Let judgment come upon the rest. They've been given warning after warning after warning, and now they will know I do not give idle threats."

Theologians tell us that the mark on the forehead was the Hebrew letter *taw*, because that letter is the one that resembles a cross. A warring angel, clothed in linen, puts that mark on the intercessors' foreheads to protect them. God specifically says, "Do not let judgment touch My intercessors; do not let it touch My righteous remnant. Angel, protect them." Angelic intervention was released through man's intercession.

Heaven's angel armies are released into the affairs of men as a result of our crying out to God. Our prayer rooms may not have many in them—only a remnant—but angels fill that room. They are attending to receive assignments. They are there to hear decrees they can assist. They are attending to bring prayers up before God and minister answers. They are there to minister protection and deliverance. Prayer time releases more angel activity than any other time.

Angels and God's Judgment on Earth

Angels bring swift judgment on nations and regions that are consumed by iniquity. Genesis 19:1 describes how two angels came to Lot in Sodom, in which the dominant sin was homosexuality. The men of the town tried to break the door down to rape these angels who appeared as men, but the angels smote them with blindness. Due to the sinful state of the region, the deep-rooted iniquities, Sodom was eventually destroyed.

Angels can break strongholds of bondage. Some things that we must break in our lives, our families, our communities, and even our nation require divine assistance. There are deep, iniquitous roots that don't want to go. The good news is, if we declare the victory of King Jesus and if we will not relent, victory will come forth. Angels will assist our decrees against cultural bondage!

Angels in Combat

Do angels fight for God's people? Absolutely. Second Kings 19:35 tells us that angels killed 185,000 soldiers who attacked the people of God. Angels are observant, engaged, warring attendants when they need to be. When necessary, they can become physically involved in a natural conflict on the earth.

Second Chronicles 20 says that angels set ambushes against the Moabite and Amorite armies that had come to fight the people of God and had them surrounded. It appeared to be a hopeless situation. The men would be killed and the women and children would be taken as slaves. The king at the time was Jehoshaphat. As they sought the Lord with fasting and prayer, the prophet Jahaziel prophesied, "You will not have to fight this battle—the battle is the Lord's." How was the battle the Lord's? God sent the angel armies to set ambushes against the enemy. It is in this chapter where you see the famous story in which Jehoshaphat sent the praisers first to march against the Amorite armies. It's as though God said, "You send the choirs; I'll send the angels." Angels began to ambush as the people of God praised, worshiped, and marched forward.

Revelation 12 shows us that angels can also be involved in spiritual conflicts, not just physical or natural ones:

Then there was war in heaven. Michael and his angels fought against the dragon and his angels. And the dragon lost the battle, and he and his angels were forced out of heaven. This great dragon—the ancient serpent called the devil, or Satan, the one deceiving the whole world—was thrown down to the earth with all his angels. Then I heard a loud voice shouting across the heavens, "It has come at last—salvation and power and the Kingdom of our God, and the authority of his Christ. For the accuser of our brothers and sisters has been thrown down to earth—the one who accuses them before our God day and night. And they have defeated him by the blood of the Lamb and by their testimony. And they did not love their lives so much that they were afraid to die (Revelation 12:7-11 NLT).

Michael and his angels fought against the dragon and his angels and won. Assisting us are angels who are more powerful than Lucifer and his angels. Lucifer and his angels fought, but they didn't win. Angels fight for God's people and His purpose. They are victorious warriors. Angels can fight spiritual battles for us in the heavenlies when it's necessary. Whether the fight is over a nation, region, town, or cultural condition, angels can help us fight in the natural realm or the spiritual.

During the Six Day War in 1967, angels were involved in the natural conflict in Israel during the war with Syria and the surrounding nations. I have heard of many UFO sightings during those days. Perhaps it wasn't UFOs, but UFAs—angels. The enemy army saw battalions of tanks and huge warriors marching against them that no one else could see. I believe it was the angel Michael and his angels protecting Israel as God had commissioned them. Yes, angels fight for God's people.

Angels Go Before Us

Angels go before us to open doors for us. In Exodus 23:20, God told Moses and his people just as they are about to leave the land of Egypt and go to their Promised Land, *"Behold, I send an Angel before thee, to keep thee in the way, and to bring thee into the place which I have prepared."*

Exodus 23:23 says, *"For mine Angel shall go before thee, and bring thee in unto the Amorites, and the Hittites, and the Perizzites, and the*

Canaanites, the Hivites, and the Jebusites: and I will cut them off." The captain of angel armies, Lord Sabaoth depicted here, has the angels go before us to lead us to a place that is prepared for us, cutting off the strategies of our enemies.

Prepared is the Hebrew word *kuwn* used 25 times in the Old Testament to refer to a dynasty. It means "to set in order, made ready, or a firm, established, fixed, and steadfast place of existence" (Strong, H3559). A dynasty references a king and his family ruling over a region, territory, or nation. God sends angels to bring us to a prepared place, an ordained place that He wants us to rule. Why? So He can establish His dynasty there.

The dynasty of the Kingdom of God that we extend in Jesus' name is prepared for advancement by angels. Angels help things come into alignment so the Kingdom can be established locally, regionally, and worldwide. Without angels, we cannot do all that the Kingdom of God needs to do in our territory. We are here to rule and reign in Christ's name. We are here to extend the jurisdiction of our God. Most certainly we have authority to do that through prayers and decrees in Christ's name that align with God's Word. If the people of God arise and boldly declare God's Word into their regions, angels will go before them to open up the opportunities as well as cut off the adversaries against it. Angels are sent to assist the church (*ekklesia*) in extending God's kingdom throughout the earth.

The prepared place that's talked about in Exodus 23:23 was occupied by enemies. Our prepared place is also occupied. Enemies occupy the territories all around us. Every time we try to do something there are enemies of the Kingdom of God who try to resist it and stop us from going forward. The promise is that God will send His angels before us to cut them off. I have no doubt that we are doing what we are doing in the state of Ohio because angels are assisting us right now in cutting off demon powers. We are here to declare God's dynasty and to represent the rule of Jesus Christ! We have received a steadfast place of existence where we can represent our King, and angels are going before us to open doors of opportunity to us so that we can establish the Kingdom of God. To me, this is simply New Testament Christianity.

Second Chronicles 32:21 says concerning Syria, "*The Lord sent an angel which cut off all the mighty men of valour.*" An angel was sent ahead to cut off the enemy warriors. I believe the angels are being sent before us to cut off the enemies and open up our regions.

In Genesis 24:7, Abraham told his servant to go to his homeland to find a bride for his son Isaac, saying, "The Lord will send His angel before you and He will see to it you find a bride there." Angels go before us to prepare Holy Spirit connections. Here you see that they can even lead you to the right person to marry. This angel brought Abraham's servant, without a GPS or a cell phone, to a well where Rebekah was drawing water in another country hundreds of miles away! Why not expect to see these supernatural connections in our times? We are heirs and it's one of our benefits.

Genesis 24:40 says that Abraham's servant told Rebekah's brother Laban about the prophetic word from Abraham that said, "*The Lord...will send His angel with you and prosper your way*" (NKJV). *Prosper* is the Hebrew word *tsaleach,* which means "profitable, prosperous, prosperity, or to break out" (Strong, H6743). God sends angels before us to break us out of confinement or constraints into prosperity. It is time for the New Testament church and Christ's heirs to shift from lack into supernatural prosperity. Angels are here to help us do that. They are here to cut off poverty and prosper our way.

In 1984, the Oasis Church, where I still pastor today, was in need of a new sanctuary. The building we were in, which is now our education building, was too small. At the time we were doubling in attendance about every six months. We began to raise the funds for the down payment, about a quarter of a million dollars, and had talked with a bank that seemed to be favorable to us.

One Sunday morning during this process a fascinating event took place. We were in a 21-day period of fasting and praying for breakthrough for the new building. The praise and worship on this day just kept going higher and higher as God's presence seemed so near. The old sanctuary had three double doors in the back, one set on each end and one in the middle. As I looked out from the platform, suddenly three angels appeared, one at each set of doors. They looked like they were huge beings of bright light. Frankly, I was astounded. I had never seen anything like this before. As I looked on in amazement, a bold word of faith rose up from my spirit and I began to declare, "God has sent His angels and we have gotten victory. We are going to build that building!" We shouted, we decreed, and we worshiped with all our heart. It was amazing.

The next day, however, was not so amazing. That Monday, 71 savings and loans in Ohio shut down in one of the worst banking crises our state has ever seen. The bank we were working with was one of them. Here I've declared great victory. I've declared angels are helping us and our bank has closed down. Though we had raised the down payment, it appeared no loan for a new building was going to happen. I was confused and it looked impossible. To say I wondered what was happening is an understatement.

I began to pray, saying, "Lord, I know I saw Your angels at the back doors. I know You've sent them to assist us. You said You've given us victory. So what's happening?"

That Thursday I received a call from the president of the bank we were working with to get the loan. The bank president is a strong Christian. He said, "Pastor, come and get your two million dollar loan."

I said, "What! How? You're shut down!"

He said, "I'll explain when you get here. Just come and sign the note today so I can record it." Of course, I got in the car and drove straight there thinking I'm either crazy and hearing things or God's up to something!

When I arrived the bank president told me that indeed they were being forced to merge with a larger bank because of the crisis. But he said because of his institution's profitability he had asked the governor to give them 24 hours to deal with any unfinished business. For some reason the governor granted the request and his bank was the only one given this extension. He said, "You are unfinished business. Sign the documents and build that sanctuary."

I'm not sure how all that happened. But I believe there were three large angels in the governor's office saying, "You can close 70 banks today, but you're giving this one 24 more hours." I have no doubt the angels sent to our aid broke confinement and shifted events in our favor. God gave us supernatural victory as promised. We have now preached the Gospel around the world many times from that sanctuary. Our God is awesome!

Angels and Prophetic Words

In Judges 13 an angel came to Manoah and his wife. She was barren, but the angel said they were going to have a son. He even told her what she was to eat and drink. The prophetic word came to pass, and she did have a son and named him Samson.

In the often read Christmas story, Mary was given a prophetic word. The angel Gabriel said, "You're going to have the prophesied Messiah." Gabriel even repeated the prophecy of Isaiah 7:14 to Mary, "*A virgin shall conceive, and bear a son.*" The angel knew the prophetic word and he was bringing it to pass.

First Timothy 1:18 says that prophetic words are to be used as warfare strategies. I have used this all over the state of Ohio. When I hold prayer assemblies in one of our 88 counties, I start with prophetic words to our region. This sparks faith for breakthrough. Also, Judges 13:3 shows us that angels help those prophetic words come to pass. What vital assistance! I have no doubt angels have done that for us in Ohio. Angels have helped us overcome Jezebel and religious spirits that have caused great barrenness in the past. Angels have partnered with us in shifting Ohio from a spiritually dry desert to one ripe for revival. Great revival is now being stirred throughout our region because of promises God's people have been decreeing in every county and over 600 churches. Angels have been hearkening to those prophetic words and warring alongside of us for their fulfillment.

Many of us have been given prophetic words. If you have received a prophetic word, decree it in the name of the Lord. Angels are here to assist in bringing prophetic promises to pass. Many of the prophetic promises that have come to you are not going to happen without angelic assistance. We have to decree, pray, and loose them.

Angels Enlighten and Reveal

Daniel 8:16 says that Daniel heard a voice saying, "*Gabriel, make this man understand the vision*" (ESV). In other words, "Gabriel, explain this to him." As Gabriel approached, Daniel fell on his face as the angel revealed the future to Daniel, explaining that what he had heard was about the end times.

Mary, Joseph, and Zechariah were also told by angels what was going to happen in the future. The point is clear that angels can come and reveal future times and events to us. In Zechariah 1:9, Zechariah had a dream about different colored horses. He asked the angel who was talking to him about it, "What does this mean?" The angel said, "I'll show you what it means." That is, of course, revelation. Angels give revelation and enlightenment to heirs. They can show us things to come.

Angels and Messages

Angels in the Old and New Testament give messages. The Hebrew word for angel is *malakh,* and the Greek word is *aggelos.* They both have the same meaning—messengers. So it should not be surprising that they give messages.

Throughout the Scripture it references, "The angel of the Lord said..." to someone or a group of someones (Genesis 16:9; 17:1; 31:11; Judges 2:4; 5:23; 6:20; 13:13; 1 Kings 13:8; 1 Chronicles 21; Zechariah 4:1; Acts 8:26; 10:3, 7). It's not weird; it's normal Christianity. Their very name, by definition, describes angels as messengers who communicate to us.

Angels Can Strengthen Us

In 1 Kings 19, Elijah was on the run from Queen Jezebel and fled to Beersheba, hiding under a broom tree. In actuality, he was so exhausted that he passed out beneath the tree. An angel awakened him some time later and showed him a baked cake and a jar of water, encouraging him to eat and drink. Elijah arose, ate, and then fell asleep again. The angel baked more cake, drew more water, and woke him again. Once more, Elijah ate. This strengthening by the angel was so powerful that Elijah left without eating again for the next forty days and forty nights, and he ran all the way to Mount Horeb, the mountain of God. He went from complete exhaustion to divine strength. The angel strengthened him to complete his assignment.

In Matthew 4:11, the angels came and ministered to Jesus after He had been severely tempted by the devil. They gave Him strength to continue His assignment. The same thing happened at Gethsemane, which means "the place of crushing." At that time of personal crushing, when Jesus sweat great drops of blood, angels came and ministered to Him. He was refreshed and empowered to fulfill His mission. Like Elijah and Jesus Christ, we too must have divine strength to finish the assignments before us.

Back in 2002, I received strength to continue a God assignment. I had been through about six months of intense spiritual warfare and had become very tired. During those months I had spent many nights in prayer out by the lake. I was battling Jezebel—religious, lying, and critical spirits—and I knew it.

After one of those all-night prayer times, I had appointments the next morning. I came home at daylight, got in the shower, and was getting ready. I was so tired I could hardly move. I remember standing and looking out a window upstairs and saying, "God, You have to strengthen me for today. I don't know if I can make it anymore." I had become so tired I really couldn't even pray. While looking out the window, I raised my hands in worship, and for some reason I determined I wasn't going to let my arms down until they just fell. Looking back, I still don't know why I did that, but I did, straining to hold them up to God. Just as I could not hold my arms up any longer and they started to fall, I felt two hands grab my wrists and hold them up. Somehow I knew that was the angels who had been assigned to my life when I accepted the apostolic calling in Indianapolis. As soon as they grabbed my arms, strength shot through my entire body like a super shot of adrenaline. My mind cleared and I felt like I had slept twelve hours. Strength was instantly infused into me and I heard these words, *"Do not defend yourself. God will defend and vindicate you. If you defend yourself, you will lose."*

I knew I was going to pass through my own Gethsemane, the place of crushing. Gethsemane was the place where the olives were put into huge wooden vats and they would trample on them until all of the oil was out. One of the things they made with that olive oil was anointing oil. Understanding became clear and I knew I was about to be squeezed like I had never been squeezed before. I knew I was going to be alone, praying through the nights many more times in spiritual battle. I was going to be tested (squeezed) spiritually, emotionally, physically, and mentally. And I was. I preached for the next three years without "feeling" the anointing. I did it by faith. I did it because I knew it was right. I had to trust that somehow I would be strengthened to continue. I also knew Holy Spirit was entrusting me with an assignment and I would have to trust Him through Gethsemane. I would have to trust Him when friends and family betrayed, when falsely accused, when lied about and sworn at, when isolated and alone.

It was a test that I was determined by God's grace to pass through, and rest and strength came because I knew it was a requirement for getting the oil for a new assignment. I had to trust God's Word that He would defend and vindicate. He would strengthen me for the assignment, and He has. I was trampling out a vat of anointing oil for a new assignment.

I had to overcome where others had failed to overcome in my region. So many have run from Jezebel and religious spirits. Would I run or let God squeeze the oil out? Anointing for some assignments does not come easy. It doesn't come without great testing. Yes, I had to trust God but that's not what it was about. It was about whether or not He could trust me.

I had to learn that without Holy Spirit I can do nothing. Apostolic calling is not about me, it's Christ and His Kingdom. I had to learn that I am a servant son here to give Him glory. Real joy, peace, and fulfillment comes by giving Him all the glory. Pride and ego have to be laid aside if you're going to walk as an apostle of the Lord Jesus Christ. You can't do it any other way. Anointing gets poured out on those who will agree that He gets all of the glory.

My assignment has become being one of those who are battling to open up a region for a new campaign of Jesus and battling to stop the demon campaign. It's an assignment of awakening and reformation. I am believing, praying, and working for a fresh outpouring of the Holy Spirit. I am working, praying, and strategizing for the years the locusts, the palmer worm, and the cankerworm have eaten away to be restored.

God was asking to me to make a stand in a region where people had run from Jezebel time and time again. I knew that if I didn't run, God would strengthen me for the assignment. It hasn't been easy, but ease has nothing to do with it. It is required of soldiers that they be found faithful. It's not talent or ability. It's a matter of choice. I can obey—anybody can obey—and if you fail, you receive grace and you just keep trying. In difficult times I have learned that the anointing on an overcomer is the purest anointing that there is, if God keeps getting the glory.

The early church in the book of Acts saw a lot of angel activities. The New Testament church today should be experiencing the same. Angels should be communicating to us and giving us messages. This is God's plan for His church's success in their regions. There are many today in the body of Christ who freely say what the devil has been telling them, but if you say what the angels have been telling you, they think that's weird. This must stop. We must embrace angel assistance. Let's be clear—listening to demons is weird. Listening to angels is normal Christianity.

chapter ten

MOBILIZING ANGELS
WITH YOUR WORDS

Bless the Lord, O my soul: and all that is within me, bless his holy name. Bless the Lord, O my soul, and forget not all his benefits: who forgiveth all thine iniquities; who healeth all thy diseases; who redeemeth thy life from destruction; who crowneth thee with lovingkindness and tender mercies; who satisfieth thy mouth with good things; so that thy youth is renewed like the eagle's (Psalm 103:1-5).

Bless the Lord, you His angels, who excel in strength, who do His word, heeding the voice of His word. Bless the Lord, all you His hosts [angel armies] (Psalm 103:20-21 NKJV).

The angelic assistance that we need in heaven is quite different than the angelic assistance we need now. For example, we won't need angels to protect or deliver us when we get to heaven. In fact, 1 Corinthians 6:3 says we are going to be judging angels there. *Judge* is the Greek word *krino* and it means "to decide or to give opinions as to what is right or wrong" (Strong, G2919). In heaven we are going to describe to angels what is right or what is wrong. That our judgment will give insight to angels shows our positioning as Christ's heirs. But on this side of heaven we need angels who excel in strength, perform God's Word, bring God's promises to pass, and assist us in our position of reigning with Christ on the earth.

Romans 5:17 declares that we are to reign in life. We cannot reign in life to the degree that we should unless angels assist us. Psalm 103:21 says that angels do God's good pleasure. *Pleasure* is the Hebrew word *ratson*. It means "good will, desire, inclination, grace and favor" (Strong, H7522). *Ratson* means "concrete reaction of a superior to an inferior." Jesus the King is superior. He has far more authority than we do and reigns in far greater measure. But in His name believers can reign in life. Angels are sent to help Christ's heirs do exactly that.

Angels Minister Favor

Proverbs 14:35 says, "*The king's favour is toward a wise servant: but his wrath is against him that causeth shame.*" The King's good will—or favor, *ratson*—is toward us and it is grace given. It is also administered, in some ways, by angels. The angels minister the good will of Jesus to us in *concrete* ways, not phantom ways. King Jesus, the superior one, has commanded the angel armies to do His good pleasure toward you and me. It's a rock-solid promise in our lives. It's a benefit that King David sings about in Psalm 103:2 that we are to never forget. Don't forget that angels are assigned to minister God's good will to you in real ways.

The Hebrew idea behind *ratson* is "concrete." It solidly materializes. *Concrete* involves union with something that is material or actual and it means "cohesion to form a mass."[1] King David says angels are amassing God's good will that is *solidly real* to materialize and adhere or stick to us. The good will of Christ sticks with you. It's not fragile or hit and miss. It is something you can stand on because it's concrete. Angels cause the blessings of God to materialize in concrete ways.

King David says God's favor toward His heirs is sticky. It's a sticky benefit. If I were to have a jar of honey and pour someone a handful of it, you would find out it's sticky. God's favor is sticky! Have you ever met someone who is "sticky" with favor? It just seems all they do is blessed. That is how God wants all His heirs to live. He wants all His benefits sticking to them and working His good pleasure. *Benefit* is the Hebrew word *gemuwl*. It means "to reward or to treat well" (Strong, H1576). A business that provides benefits to its employees does so to treat them well. Most certainly God treats His heirs, the born-again ones, very well. We are His heirs and His angels are sent to reward us with tangible material blessings that are concrete.

Psalm 103:20 says angels "*do his commandments, hearkening unto the voice of his word.*" When God's Word is decreed (voiced) by the heirs, angels hearken to them. They organize to bring it to pass. God created the angels in such a way that they hearken to what His Word decrees. We have to understand that if we don't give voice to God's Word on the earth, then angels have no voice on the earth to hearken to, unless God sovereignly speaks or it's a predetermined Word of God that He has already given. In Matthew 16:19 Jesus said, "*And I will give unto thee the keys of the kingdom of heaven: and whatsoever thou shalt bind on earth shall be bound in heaven: and whatsoever thou shalt loose on earth shall be loosed in heaven.*" The authority to bind and loose is given to believers in Jesus' name. Angels are loosed in heaven and we are to loose them on the earth.

Many today, I believe, are missing out on some awesome benefits because they are not giving voice to God's Word. Often, they are voicing anything and everything *except* God's Word. The angels are waiting for you to say things that loose them. The key is to speak the Word of God. The reason that much of the body of Christ today sees more demonic activity than angel activity is because they activate more demons than they do angels. It's amazing to me how conditioned and accepting much of the body of Christ is today to demonic strategies and activities. It's almost as though the body of Christ expects demons to move against them. They expect the kingdom of hell to fight them at every turn. They expect hell's obstacles and hindering demons. Yes, we know demons are here to steal, kill, and destroy. Why not renew our minds to the fact that we have far more assisters helping us to win than we have resisters who are causing us to lose? Why not expect Holy Spirit and His angels to come to our aid? Why not expect angel armies to have a better strategy than demons have? Why not expect our leader, Jesus, and His angels to be more powerful and wiser than fallen angels that were dumb enough to follow Lucifer? Our angels thought God was more powerful than Lucifer. Why not decree and expect the Kingdom of Almighty God to surround us with protection and deliverance? Why shouldn't the church expect more angelic activity than demonic activity?

It's time to recondition our minds to truth and reposition our thoughts. It's time to get up in the morning looking for angels instead of demons. Yes, demons and hell's kingdom are real, but so are angels and our Kingdom. Our angels are stronger and smarter than hell's demons, and we have more of them. But far more than that, our God, our King, our Lord is exceedingly, abundantly, above and beyond, more powerful than Lucifer ever thought about being. It's time to act like it and stop thinking in line with our fallen nature. We aren't fallen anymore. We are born again heirs. It's time to believe and stop thinking like unrighteous sinners and start thinking like the heirs of God. The culture of defeat that has been propagated by the body of Christ for decades is delusional. It makes no sense biblically. We aren't fallen down wimps who are demon dominated. We are seated with Christ in heavenly places. We are heirs with authority to rule and reign. Loose your angels! Expect angel armies fighting on your side! Expect to win!

Sadly, much of the body of Christ in our time expects to lose. They expect that we are not going to change this nation. They expect things are going to get worse and hell's going to win or demon strategies are going to harm us. I have a different opinion. I expect the Greater One to give us strategy to overcome. I expect to win. I expect that we are going to get strategy that overcomes all the powers of the adversary. I expect angels to be loosed. It is vital that we say what God says. When our words agree with God's Word, when our conversation aligns with God's holy promises, then angels are loosed to operate in our lives and angels are mobilized to bring God's good pleasure to pass on our behalf.

Mobilizing Angels

How do you mobilize angelic armies? With words of faith that decree what God says. *Words of faith activate angels; unbelief stifles angels.* Angels are watching and listening. Daniel said they are the "watchers." They hear what we say. Angels want to assist the high priestly ministry of Jesus and His Holy Spirit in our lives, but they sometimes have to simply fold their wings and look on because unbelief has stopped their assignment. I wonder how many times we have prayed and confessed God's Word and the angels activate to bring it to real manifestation in our lives and then, for whatever reason, we faint. We begin to doubt and disagree with the Word of God with our own words and conversations. And because of what we say the angels have to lay the assignment down undone. I wonder if there aren't some Christians who give their angels whiplash because they change so much. They "loose" their angels by declaring what God promises and then a few minutes later they say, "Oh, nothing is going to happen. This won't work. I doubt anything's going to change." Their fears produce words that cancel angelic assistance.

When angels talk to one another I have often wondered if they bring us up. I wonder if they say, "My guy doesn't seem to be able to make up his mind. He leaves the church so positive, but he usually cancels my assignments by Monday morning. Sometimes he cancels them before he even gets home. He wants God's good Kingdom benefits, but all he talks about is the dark kingdom and I can't help him." We miss awesome Kingdom benefits when we don't speak the Word of God. We certainly miss out on angels assisting God's Word to come to pass. While we have not been given authority to command angels to do whatever we want them to do (we have to have Scripture and biblical principle behind it), they are listening. Words we speak in agreement with God's Word, which we do not negate, activate angels to begin to amass the good will and concrete benefits of God in our lives. Promises can materialize when we stand in faith.

Idle Words, Idle Angels

Holy Spirit emphasized to me years ago a simple phrase: *Idle words, idle promises. Idle words, idle angels.* Jesus said:

> *How can you, being evil, speak good things? For out of the abundance of the heart the mouth speaks. A good man out of the good treasure of his heart brings forth good things, and an evil man out of the evil treasure brings forth evil things. But I say to you that for every idle word men may speak, they will give account of it in the day of judgment. For by your words you will be justified, and by your words you will be condemned* (Matthew 12:34-37 NKJV).

That is a powerful and yet sobering statement. *Idle* is the Greek word *argos* meaning "inactive, unemployed, useless, barren, nonworking, unprofitable" (Strong, G692). Jesus said we will answer for all of our useless negative words. Idle words cause promises and angels to be nonworking in our lives. Negative words are unprofitable and unproductive and bring about a forfeiture of Kingdom benefits. Negative thoughts of the heart will proceed from your mouth, causing promises to become barren. We must learn to put our angels to work with our words. We must loose them by declaring God's Word and not backing down. Bold declarations of faith deploy angels who become engaged on our behalf. Words of faith activate them to make God's promises concrete realities.

Jesus said in Matthew 12:37, *"By thy words thou shalt be justified, and by thy words thou shalt be condemned." Justified* is the Greek word *dikaioo,* and it means to set someone forth as righteous because of receiving Jesus as Lord (Strong, G1344). We have rights and privileges that are due us as born-again heirs of Christ. *Dikaioo* also means "to cause to become, to make free, or to free." Your words make for your quality of life. They "life" or "un-life" you. They free promises. The root word of *dikaioo* is *dike,* and it means "rights that are self-evident; rights that are common-sensibly ours as heirs." *Dike* is also the Greek word for justice (Strong, G1349). If we want our just rights as citizens of God's Kingdom, if we want our self-evident rights as God's heirs, then we must speak words of life and faith. Angels assigned to us will help those rights become reality. They will work to free them.

If we speak negative words of unbelief, words that disagree with God's Word, words that are contrary to the rights we are due, then Jesus adds, *"By your words you are condemned." Condemned* is the Greek word *katadikazo* and it means "to sentence, judgment, or to pronounce a sentence" (Strong, G2613). Your words sentence you to live what you say. What you speak can bind your life or loose it. You can sentence yourself to very few promises of God ever materializing in your life and you can sentence very little angelic activity from ever happening in your life by your words. Are you sentencing your life to live in lack, poverty, depression, sickness, disease, hopelessness, fear, defeat? Those things are already bound in heaven. Whatever is bound in heaven, Jesus says, we can keep from happening here. Use your authority and words of faith. Angels are waiting for you to release your authority. They are listening. Don't idle the angels with idle words. Speak words of faith at the mountain in your way, and angels will begin to cause the promise of God to begin to materialize in your life.

Jesus said in Mark 11:23 concerning faith in God, *"For assuredly, I say to you, whoever says to this mountain, 'Be removed and be cast into the sea,' and does not doubt in his heart, but believes that those things he says will be done, he will have whatever he says"* (NKJV). That phrase was not coined by Normal Vincent Peale or Dr. Kenneth Hagin. Jesus said it. *He will have whatever he says.* What a powerful key to living life as an overcomer. You're sentenced to live what you say in faith or what you speak in unbelief.

When you put all the Greek tenses of Matthew 16:19 together, it says: "Whatever you at any time encounter of hell's council that I am determined My church will prevail against, you will then face a decision as to whether you will or will not bind it or will or will not loose it. What transpires is conditional to your response. If you do purposely and consciously involve yourself in binding or loosing the issue on earth, you will find at that future moment when you do, it is already bound or it is already loosed in heaven." Jesus said it is conditional to your response. You can bind things from your life or you can loose things from heaven into your life or you could be idle and do nothing. Your motor could be running, yet you're not in gear as a Christian. Many Christians are just idling; they are going nowhere and doing nothing. We can respond in powerful authoritative faith words that agree with God's Word or we can speak our doubts. The question is, "Are you sentencing your life to cursing or loosing blessings? Life or death? Victory or defeat? Benefits or forfeiture of benefits?" There are mighty angels available to assist you as God's heir.

Don't idle your angels with idle words. Angels are waiting, hovering, circling, and listening for you to speak God's Word.

Years ago when I was sharing some of these principles, there were some young men in the youth group who decided to have an all-night prayer meeting. They were excited about the angels and what I had been teaching. One of the young men gave a testimony of what happened that night. Toward the midnight hour, they had prayed for quite a while and had been worshiping when he looked up and saw an angel standing in the back. He didn't know what to do and the angel just kept looking at him. He said finally the angel gave him a look that said, "Give me something to do!" The young men started making decrees, and all of a sudden the angel was gone! Angels are wanting to activate your words aligned with God's purposes. The church today has millions of angels available. We need to give them plenty to do. We need to put them on assignment with decrees of faith.

Are there promises, principles, or benefits you have been requesting that have not materialized in your life? If so, take heed to the words of Jesus. You have what you say. Speak words of blessing over your life and mobilize angels.

NOTE

1. *Webster's Ninth New Collegiate Dictionary* (Springfield, MA: Merriam-Webster's Inc. Publishers, 1984), s.v. "concrete."

chapter eleven

ANGELS CONNECT US TO GREAT PROSPERITY

If we believe that the devil and the kingdom of darkness can hinder the blessings of God from entering our lives, then why wouldn't we believe that Christ's angels can assist in releasing them? How can those who proclaim to be Christians believe the devil is capable of actions of which God's angels are not capable? If the heavenly hosts are connected to a giving God, then why wouldn't we believe they have the ability to release blessings upon us? The Scriptures are clear—angels avidly assist us in obtaining resources, finances, and other benefits to help us in establishing God's Kingdom here on the earth. This is explained in Acts 10:

> *There was a certain man in Caesarea called Cornelius, a centurion of what was called the Italian Regiment, a devout man and one who feared God with all his household, who gave alms generously to the people, and prayed to God always. About the ninth hour of the day he saw clearly in a vision an angel of God coming in and saying to him, "Cornelius!"*

And when he observed him, he was afraid, and said, "What is it, lord?"

So he said to him, "Your prayers and your alms have come up for a memorial before God. Now send men to Joppa, and send for Simon whose surname is Peter. He is lodging with Simon, a tanner, whose house is by the sea. He will tell you what you must do." And when the angel who spoke to him had departed, Cornelius called two of his household servants and a devout soldier from among those who waited on him continually. So when he had explained all these things to them, he sent them to Joppa (Acts 10:1-8 NKJV).

Angels connect God's people to places, people, events, businesses, sales, and material property that will prosper them. It is a part of the angels' assignment where born-again ones, heirs of Christ, are concerned. It's a fascinating principle all over the Old and New Testament that is rarely ever mentioned or taught. It's a magnificent benefit that we are told we should not ever forget. And as always, we must see it from the Scriptures and not from the televangelist version. Money is not the root of all evil. First Timothy 6:10 says, *"The love of money is the root of all evil."* Coveting money in unrighteous ways produces evil. God wants you to have money. There is no Scripture that says that we are to take a vow of poverty; in fact, it's quite the opposite. We are to expect supernatural and abundant blessings. We need money to properly function in life and society. God wants us to be a success and financially secure, but He also wants you to steward that financial resource wisely.

In Acts 10, an angel appears to a gentile, a Roman army officer of the Italian regiment by the name of Cornelius. When the angel appeared to him, he made note of Cornelius' prayer life and financial stewardship. Of all the things an angel might address, someone's giving record would not seem to be a priority. But the angel said to

Cornelius in Acts 10:4, *"Your prayers and your alms have come up for a memorial before God"* (NKJV).

Hear and Remember

The Greek word for "memorial," *mnemosunon*, means "a reminder, a record, to rehearse something, make mention, or to bring to remembrance" (Strong, G3422). A memorial draws your attention to something that needs to be remembered. It tells us about a life-changing event through the medium of chiseled stone. For example, the purpose of a memorial stone is to bring to our remembrance someone we may have forgotten.

In referring to Cornelius' memorial, the Angel of the Lord says, "Cornelius, your giving record has come up before God and it has His attention. It has been talked about in the throne room, Cornelius. God is rehearsing your giving history. Your offerings have been remembered before God." Then the angel said to him, "I want you to send men to Joppa and ask for the apostle Peter to come to your house." You might remember from past chapters that the Holy Spirit had already promised Peter that three men were going to come looking for him. Upon their arrival, Peter was instructed to follow the three men without question or doubt.

Peter continued with them to Cornelius' house, where he preached the Gospel of salvation through faith in Jesus Christ. In Acts 10:44, Luke says, *"Even as Peter was saying these things, the Holy Spirit fell upon all who were listening to the message"* (NLT). Everyone in Cornelius' house was saved and filled with the Holy Spirit. *What a blessing.* It's an eternal blessing of far greater value than any other blessing. It is because of Cornelius' prayers and offerings that angels were able to work in his life and his family's life. His offerings got the attention of God and His angels, who are sent forth to minister to the heirs of salvation. As Christians, we must understand that one of the ministries of angels is to connect us to the blessings of Christ, as well as to assist in prospering us.

According to the prophet Daniel, these angels can be identified as "watchers" (Daniel 4:13, 17, 23). Finis Jennings Dake, in his version of the Annotated Bible, defines *angels* as "those who oversee the affairs of men to enable them to bring about the will of God on the earth." In other words, angels are watching for opportunities to perform God's will on behalf of His children. What is God's will? His Word is His will.

The apostle Paul reiterates this theme in 1 Timothy 5:21, where he gives Timothy instruction on how to conduct services in the church. *"I solemnly command you in the presence of God and Christ Jesus and the highest angels to obey these instructions without taking sides or showing favoritism to anyone"* (NLT). This passage reveals that angels are watchers in our church services, waiting to be involved in what we do, what we pray, or decrees of faith we make. Essentially, they watch to see if God's will is being pursued. If it is, they work to see it come to pass. Remember, angels assist based upon hearing the Word of God that we believe and speak forth (Psalm 103:20).

Covenant Watchers

The Godhead and the holy angels do not stop watching during times when tithes and offerings are received. God and His angels continue to watch in order to see if covenant is going to be honored by the heirs. If it is, angels are loosed to connect blessings to homes and vocations. They are loosed to make us sticky with favor. If covenant is not honored, angels are simply not mobilized to assist. It's as though their hands are tied. We must obey the Word of God if we want angels to connect us to biblical prosperity. They are covenant watchers circling us to administer God's good pleasure in our lives.

God takes pleasure in your prosperity. We see this in Psalm 35:27, where King David says, *"Let the Lord be magnified, which hath pleasure in the prosperity of his servant."* The conclusion is that God wants you to prosper and has assigned His angels to assist in the development of that prosperity. It is an amazing benefit only Christ's heirs are qualified to receive.

Jesus says in Matthew 6:4 that God will return your generosity openly. "Do not give your offerings before men to be seen of men. That way the Father who sees in secret will reward you openly." *Reward* is the Greek word *apodidomi,* which means "to give back more, to sell, to repay, or restore" (Strong, G591). The God who sees gives back more than is given. He will loose restoration to heirs who honor His Word. If needed, He can cause goods, properties, or animals to sell. He can connect buyers to goods or services His children are providing. He can connect clients to His heirs. He can cause your sales to go up. And He often uses His angels to assist in accomplishing this awesome benefit. They can connect you to people, places, or things that prosper you with much more than you gave.

In Mark 12, we find Jesus observing offerings:

Jesus sat down near the collection box in the Temple and watched as the crowds dropped in their money. Many rich people put in large amounts. Then a poor widow came and dropped in two small coins. Jesus called his disciples to him and said, "I tell you the truth, this poor widow has given more than all the others who are making contributions. For they gave a tiny part of their surplus, but she, poor as she is, has given everything she had to live on" (Mark 12:41-44 NLT).

Why did Jesus watch the collection box? To see if He could loose the covenant blessings God had willed for His widowed daughter openly, before the eyes of men. To reward her generosity, Jesus teaches

His people in His own words that He "watches" to prosper us. It is His will that His children prosper and be in health, even as their souls prosper (3 John 2). To enforce this awesome promise of the Godhead, He assigns angels to watch for ways to minister "purposed prosperity." They are looking for ways to honor covenant. They are watching to see to whom they can release blessing.

Although some may wish that the Kingdom of heaven closed its eyes during offerings, Scripture teaches us the opposite. They watch, not to bring condemnation or harsh judgment, but rather to have grounds upon which to bless us. Angels are not attempting to catch those walking in disobedience. That is not their assignment. They are looking to honor the covenant and identify those upon whom they can loose covenant blessings. This brings revelation to Acts 20:35, *"Remember the words of the Lord Jesus, how he said, It is more blessed to give than to receive."* How is that possible? Because the value of the reward is greater than the value of the gift.

Christ desires to connect you to blessings. Jesus said in Luke 6:38, *"Give, and you will receive. Your gift will return to you in full—pressed down, shaken together to make room for more, running over, and poured into your lap. The amount you give will determine the amount you get back"* (NLT). If you use a thimble to measure your giving, a thimble is what will be used to measure your return. If you use a shovel, a shovel is what will be used to measure your return. He is making an amazing promise to us when He says, "Give and it will be given to you; give and you will receive." His promise couldn't be clearer. You cannot out-give God. It's a law of the Kingdom and angels will help to fulfill it.

The Principle of Giving and Receiving

After thirty-five years of ministry, I've found that the number one reason people do not give tithes or offerings to the Lord is they don't believe what Jesus has promised. On what do I base this? It is the only logical conclusion at which one can arrive. If you are going to get more in return and God has guaranteed it, then why would you refrain from giving? The apostle Paul writes in 2 Corinthians 9:6, *"He which soweth sparingly shall reap also sparingly; and he which soweth bountifully shall reap also bountifully."* Bounty comes through sowing. We see this again in Proverbs, where it says, *"Honor the Lord with your wealth and with the best part of everything you produce. Then he will fill your barns with grain, and your vats will overflow with good wine"* (Proverbs 3:9-10 NLT). This is reiterated in Moffatt's Translation of Proverbs 11:24-25 which says, *"One gives away, and still he grows the richer: another keeps what he should give, and is the poorer. A liberal soul will be enriched, and he who waters will himself be watered."* The Living Bible says, *"It is possible to give away and become richer! It is also possible to hold on too tightly and lose everything. Yes, the liberal man shall be made rich! By watering others, he waters himself."* The Bible clearly teaches that when we sow, we also reap. There's no ambiguity in this promise whatsoever. For if we give, it is guaranteed we shall receive. When we release what is in our hands, God releases what is in His hands.

"The angel of the Lord went up from Gilgal to Bokim and said to the Israelites, 'I brought you out of Egypt into this land that I swore to give your ancestors, and I said I would never break my covenant with you.'" (Judges 2:1 NLT). The promise to God's people is bold. The captain of angel armies and the angels themselves will never break covenant with you. The covenant will be honored. Covenant rights, provided by the cross of Christ, will be respected by the angels. They are waiting to help lead you into promised blessings.

Offerings and the release of great blessings by angels are mentioned throughout the Scriptures. In Judges 6, the Angel of the Lord called Gideon, a mighty man of valor, to step out of his comfort zone and into a place of battle. The Midianites came every year and stole Israel's harvest, leaving the entire nation impoverished. The Angel of the Lord appeared to Gideon and said, "You are a mighty man of valor. I want you to stop the raiding of the harvest against Israel." Out of obedience, Gideon prepared an offering and told the angel to stay there while he went to give his offering to the Lord, and the angel did exactly that. A few hours later, Gideon brought back a young, cooked goat and some bread. As he placed his offering before the Lord, the angel appeared and said, "Pour the broth over it," so Gideon did as he was instructed. When he finished, the Angel of the Lord touched the offering with his staff and fire shot out and consumed it. Then the angel disappeared.

Notice, Gideon gave an offering. I do not know what a goat cost in those days, but it cost something. There was a value to that goat. I don't know what bread cost in those days, but it cost him something—especially in a time of famine. But I do know, when he gave an offering a great breakthrough occurred. Seven years of lost harvest was restored and great victory was obtained. *Harvest*, by definition, means "success, prosperity, or abundance." First an offering was given, then success was loosed. First an offering was given, then prosperity was loosed. First an offering was given, then harvest was restored.

Angels Carry Breakthrough Blessings

In Judges 13, remember an angel appeared to Samson's parents. He spoke to Samson's mother, "Even though you have not been able to have children, you are going to have a son." When the angel appeared later to Samson's father, Manoah, he said the same thing. Manoah answered, "Stay here while I go get an offering."

The angel replied, "I'll stay and you can prepare an offering, but I'm not going to eat it."

Manoah asked, "What's your name?"

And the angel said, "It is too deep, too wonderful for you—you wouldn't understand." Some translations say his name was *Wonderful* or *Wonder*. Perhaps he was an angel created to do wonders. The

Scripture says that when Manoah laid the offering upon the altar, flames shot skyward and the angel ascended into the flames.

Notice that an offering precipitated Holy Fire and angel assistance. The Angel of the Lord observed Samson's mother and father. He observed their offering to the Lord and then a great breakthrough came to their home. Barrenness was broken and Samson was born. Angels carry breakthrough anointing that blesses the home.

Malachi 3 tells us that an open heaven occurs when we bring tithes and offerings to our God. That is extremely significant where angels are concerned as it points us toward angelic blessings and prosperity. The pathways of heaven are opened for angels to begin to work and ascend and descend on us with great blessings."

> *Should people cheat God? Yet you have cheated me! But you ask, 'What do you mean? When did we ever cheat you?' You have cheated me of the tithes and offerings due to me. You are under a curse, for your whole nation has been cheating me. Bring all the tithes into the storehouse so there will be enough food [provision] in my Temple. If you do," says the Lord of heaven's armies, "I will open the windows of heaven for you. I will pour out a blessing so great you won't have enough room to take it in! Try it! Put me to the test!"* (Malachi 3:8-10 NLT)

An open heaven occurs when you bring tithes and offerings that are due Him.

Genesis 28 tells us when there is an open heaven, angels ascend and descend. He saw a ladder going up into heaven and angels ascending and descending upon it. The story reveals that a gate of heaven (some call it an open heaven) is the place where angels ascend and descend. We can conclude that when we bring tithes to the storehouse, we open gates of heaven so that angels can ascend and descend upon our lives, connecting us as heirs with rightful covenant blessings.

God said to Jacob in Genesis 28:14, *"And thy seed shall be as of the dust of the earth, thou shalt spread abroad to the west, to the east, and to the north, and to the south: and in thee and thy seed shall all the families of the earth be blessed."* There is an amazing Hebrew word that translates "spread abroad." It is the Hebrew word *parats* meaning "the breakthrough anointing." It refers to the breaker anointing on King Jesus. Micah 2:13 says, *"The Breaker [the Messiah] will go up before them. They will break through, pass in through the gate and go out through it, and their King will pass on before them, the Lord at their head"* (AMP). The word *breaker* is the same word as "spread abroad"—*parats*—and it means "to scatter and shatter, to open a new way or open new doors and new territories" (Strong, H6555). The breaker anointing of King Jesus is upon the angels who ascend and descend from paths or spheres over someone's life that the tithe has helped to open. Angels assist heirs by scattering and shattering obstacles to blessings. They break up the things that devour covenant blessings over our lives and open doors of opportunity for us. They ascend and descend where the heaven is opened, opening up doors leading to breakthroughs of great blessings.

Jehovah Jireh

Abraham, the father of our faith, lived under an open heaven. King Abimelech observed God's favor on Abraham when he said, *"God is with thee in all that thou doest"* (Genesis 21:22). In other words, "Everything you touch seems to work." Why was that? Abraham was a giver. Genesis 14:20 tells us that Abraham, 430 years before the law, gave ten percent of all to God. Tithing was never under the law. It was a covenant principle that will exist as long as there is seedtime and harvest. We are still planting seeds in the spring and harvesting in the fall. That has not stopped. It says Abraham gave a tenth of all that he had to the high priest, Melchizedek, whom the book of Hebrews describes as a type of Christ (Hebrews 5:6). In both the Old and the New Testament, the tithe is the Lord's. Abraham was one of the richest men who ever lived. By today's standards he was a billionaire and gave ten percent of everything to God.

Years later, after Isaac was born to Abraham and Sarah in their old age, God tested Abraham. In Genesis 22:2, we read, *"Take your son, your only son—yes, Isaac, whom you love so much—and go to the land of Moriah. Go and sacrifice him as a burnt offering on one of the mountains, which I will show you"* (NLT). Abraham obeyed. Just as he was about to plunge the knife into Isaac and offer him up as a sacrifice, an angel called from an open heaven saying, "Stop! Don't do that. I know now that you fear God!" At that moment, Abraham saw a ram, caught by its horns in a thicket. God had provided a substitute, just as Abraham declared to Isaac when they started up the mountain. Isaac had asked "Where's the sacrifice?" And Abraham said, "God will make one; He will provide. Don't worry." This is the picture, of course, of the sacrifice of Jesus for you and me on Calvary. I don't know how the angel tangled up the ram's horns in that thicket at just the right moment, but he did it! Genesis 22:14 says that Abraham renamed the place Jehovah Jireh, which means "the God who provides." *Jehovah Jireh, my Provider.* I am so glad I have a God who sees to it that I prosper.

Abraham lived under an open heaven because he willingly brought God his tithes and offerings. As you do the same, angels will show you the ram in the thicket, provision you did not know was there. Jehovah Jireh is the Provider and angels minister aspects of that to the heirs. The Lord will see to the provision if you open the pathway by bringing Him your tithes and offerings.

One of the promises God made Abraham was that He would bless his descendants after 400 years in Egyptian bondage. God gave a promised land to Abraham's heirs. It was a land of milk and honey, a land of great natural resources and wealth. Proverbs 13:22 says, *"The wealth of the sinner is stored up for the righteous"* (NKJV). That certainly happened to Abraham's heirs, and it happens for Christ's heirs at even greater levels.

After 400 years of Egyptian bondage, Moses led Israel through 40 years in the wilderness to the Promised Land. Exodus 23:20 recounts God's announcement, *"Behold, I send an Angel before thee, to keep thee in the way, and to bring thee into the place which I have prepared."* Angels lead us to places of promise. Exodus 23:23 says, *"For mine Angel shall go before thee, and bring thee in unto the Amorites, and the Hittites, and the Perizzites, and the Canaanites, the Hivites, and the Jebusites: and I will cut them off."* God describes these resident groups of people as sinful idolaters. Exodus 33:2 says it again, *"I will send an angel before thee."* Clearly, angels led Israel to the Promised Land and, likewise, lead us to places of great resources and breakthrough.

Angels led Israel to a place where the wealth of the sinners had been stored up for them. The Promised Land was filled with nations who were building homes, cities, and road systems. They were clearing the land for gardens, plowing fields, and pulling up weeds. They were digging wells and planting thousands of fruit trees. They were planting thousands of acres of grapevines. For whom? For the righteous to whom God was planning to give it!

The wealth of sinners is stored up for the righteous. Angels know how to connect us to this wealth, how to transfer wealth to the promised heirs. They know how to lead us to the place of inheritance and God provision prepared for us. Someone is storing up great resources for the Kingdom of God right now. It's time for the transfer of wealth. Angels are involved in the transition of bringing the wealth of the wicked to the hands of the heirs. Angels are tangling up rams in the thickets right now. They are loosing provisions.

So what's our assignment? Honor the covenant. Open those pathways and see what God will do. If you want to see angels ascend and descend into your life, blessing you, your extended family, and causing great breakthroughs to come, and if you want angels connecting you to financial provision, then honor the Word of God. Bring all the tithes to Him.

chapter twelve

MAKING
ANGELS ANGRY

Angels in the Journey

The Exodus depicts a people going from slavery to a promised land. It was a journey of freedom to the fulfillment of a dream—a land flowing with milk and honey. The promise, however, was not without conditions. Moses was given ten commandments regarding social laws, sexual laws, and rules of conduct for their journey. The book of Exodus lists these responsibilities. The Israelites could not live any way they wanted and gain the promise; obedience was required.

God ends His principles of covenant regulations with this statement:

Behold, I send an Angel before you to keep you in the way and to bring you into the place which I have prepared. Beware of Him and obey His voice; do not provoke Him, for He will not pardon your transgressions (Exodus 23:20-21 NKJV)

Let me interject here that angels do not forgive sins. There's only One who can forgive us of sin, and that's Christ Jesus, through His shed blood. That's the only way.

He will not pardon your transgressions; for My name is in Him. But if you indeed obey His voice and do all that I speak, then I will be an enemy to your enemies and an adversary to your adversaries. For My Angel will go before you and bring you in to the Amorites and the Hittites and the Perizzites and the Canaanites and the Hivites and the Jebusites; and I will cut them off (Exodus 23:21-23 NKJV).

Do Not Provoke Angels

Great authority was given to the angel mentioned in Exodus 23. He was to go ahead, leading the Israelites to a place God had prepared for them. Additionally, God gave a warning not to provoke this angel, but to give attention to and beware of him. *Beware* is the Hebrew word *shamar*, which means "to watch, observe, pay attention, guard, or regard" (Strong, H8104). The caution against provoking angels indicates that provocation is possible.

The word *provoke* in Hebrew is the word *marar*, which means "to grieve or vex" (Strong, H4843). The root is *mar*, meaning "bitterness, anger or chafing" (Strong, H4751). *Marar* is the Hebrew word for "discontent." God warns the Israelites not to cause the angels to become discontented. Again, do not anger them.

By using this word (*mar*) throughout Scripture, God gives further revelation. In Genesis 27:34, *mar* is used to describe the heart-crushing experience of a family that is in turmoil. Brothers Jacob and Esau were feuding and Jacob ultimately stole Esau's birthright. Their mother got involved. The extended family got involved. Fighting, estrangement, deception, and stealing took place. These events caused bitterness (*mar*).

God says that angels become discontent when there is fighting among the brothers. Lies and deception chafe them. Conniving or using deceit to obtain what is not rightfully yours angers the angels.

This could possibly explain the lack of victory in the church of America today. There is way too much fighting and conniving among the brothers, a constant war over things that are not rightfully theirs, which they want to take by deceitful means. Apostolates are called to confront such wrongdoing and bring change. They are called to challenge people to live in such a way that angels are content. They must confront and remove sin that is provoking the Kingdom of God.

In 1 Samuel 1:10, *mar* is used to describe the broken-heartedness of Hannah, who was barren and weeping for a baby. She was at the temple altar in prayer, sobbing for a child, when Eli heard her. In reference to angels, God used this word (*mar*) to reveal that provoking angels results in sadness. It brings us into a position of barrenness and unfruitfulness, where broken-heartedness could result.

We must guard how we live because angels are watching. They see our behavior. They observe our conduct with one another. Proper conduct provides an atmosphere through which angels can move freely and minister among us. We are responsible to provide an atmosphere for the Kingdom of God to advance. We are to cultivate the conditions for divine assistants to release blessing.

In 1 Samuel 15:32 and Job 20, *mar* is used to describe the thought of dying, being killed, or feeling like you're dying. Provoking angels will cause feelings of being unprotected and hopeless. When you live in a manner that chafes angels, you are vulnerable. In American churches today there is sometimes despair over unfulfilled promises. One reason can be an atmosphere that quenches Holy Spirit and provokes His angels. God is calling us to repent. We have to live in such a way that the Kingdom promises can truly manifest.

In Esther 4:1, *mar* is used to describe Mordecai weeping bitterly over the evil edict of the king. A wicked man named Haman convinced King Artaxerxes to sign an order that allowed the killing of any Jew at any time. That evil decree brought *mar*—bitter tears. Mordecai went to the gate, where the law was made, and wept bitterly. This is enlightening because God and His angels are provoked by decrees—by evil government rulings, laws, or edicts. The word *decree* is *dath*, meaning "laws," and this includes statutes, edicts, statements, spoken words, declarations, and phrases (Strong, H1881).

Guard Your Words

We must align ourselves with God's Word, saying what He says. We need to believe His Word is right and declare it. Job 6:25 says that right words are forcible. The Hebrew word for "forcible" is *marats* meaning "powerful or constructive" (Strong, H4834). Declaring God's Word constructs good things to come to us. Faith decrees, based on God's Word, mobilize angels to help us build successful lives. Of course, evil decrees of unbelief do the opposite. They mobilize demons to tear down or disrupt. Negative attitudes and statements are not simply harmless musings of a pessimist. They activate demons. We must realize the importance of our words and confess our faith based upon God's Word. If we will, angel armies will mobilize to cause God's promises to intersect with our paths.

In Matthew 12:37, Jesus commented that by your words you are "justified" and by your words you are "condemned." In Mark 11:23, He said you will get what you speak. When we say what God says, according to Psalm 103:20, angels harken to obey. Angels harken to the word of the Lord that we proclaim, but when we speak words contrary to His Word—when we speak unbelief, when we are negative, when we disagree with what God says—angels can be provoked. When the Hebrew word *marats* (forcible) is used in a negative way, it means to irritate. Using negative words irritates your life. They irritate your destiny. Right words construct destiny and mobilize angels.

Proverbs 18:21 says, *"Death and life are in the power of the tongue."* *The Message* reads, *"Words kill; words give life; they're either poison or fruit—you choose."* The choice is ours. We can speak our doubts or our faith. We can say what God says or what the world says. We can speak our fear or our confidence in God. Either way, there are consequences; one is good, the other bad. One looses angels and the other permits demons to operate. There are some who wonder why they see more demon activity in the church than angel activity. Perhaps it's because they activate more demons with their words than they do angels. I wonder if this isn't true in many churches. They expect demons to work against them. They expect demons to attack. And, of course, we should be alert to this and bind it in Jesus' name. *But we should expect more angel activity than demon activity.* There are more good angels than demons. It's time to loose them with words of faith aligned with God's Word. *Release angels; don't provoke them.*

The Israelites in the Exodus did not heed God's warning; rather than obey God's Word, they became disobedient, rebellious idol-worshipers. They commissioned Aaron, the high priest, to gather gold which they melted down and built into a golden calf to worship. Negativity flowed as they declared the Promised Land a "pipe dream." They murmured, griped, and complained. God's Word describes them as *decreeing an evil report.* They provoked the angel of the Lord, as God had warned them not to do. Thus, they did not inherit the Promised Land.

When Moses sent the twelve spies into the land to see how best to take it, two of them, Joshua and Caleb, returned with a favorable report. Ten of them said the Israelites would not be able to do it. In Numbers 13:32, God suggests that these ten gave an evil report. For this evil, God sentenced them to wander in the wilderness. The book of Hebrews describes those days as Days of Provocation. The

ANGEL ARMIES

Israelites persisted in this type of attitude and suffered the consequences of their wrong thinking.

The Israelites continued in unbelief. Hebrews 3 says:

Wherefore (as the Holy Ghost saith, To day if ye will hear his voice, harden not your hearts, as in the provocation, in the day of temptation in the wilderness: when your fathers tempted me, proved me, and saw my works forty years. Wherefore I was grieved with that generation, and said, They do alway err in their heart; and they have not known my ways (Hebrews 3:7-10).

I do not want to live in such a way that God would ever have to say of me, "That's just the way he is. He's pessimistic. He's always talking negatively and dwelling in unbelief. That's just him; he's bent that way."

The word *provocation* in Greek is the word *parapikrasmos*, meaning "irritation" (Strong, G3894). Wrong words irritate God's purpose. Negative words irritate your world, your health, your family, your vocation, your children, and your nation.

In the book of Hebrews, the word *parapikrasmos* is used to describe the griping, complaining, and murmuring that irritated the Lord and provoked Him against the Israelites. Also, the angels assigned to lead the people to His promise became irritated. God is not pleased when we disobey or disagree with His words. Angels are discontent and even irritated by an evil decree. Provoking angels stops them from leading us into God's promise. Truth be told, evil words of unbelief cancel angelic assignments, halting them from completing the tasks at hand.

Wandering in the Wilderness

Just like the Israelites, we can circle the wilderness again if we want to. I choose not to participate. Another translation of Hebrews 3 says:

That is why the Holy Spirit says, "Today when you hear his voice, don't harden your hearts as Israel did when they rebelled, when they tested me in the wilderness. There your ancestors tested and tried my patience, even though they saw my miracles for forty years. So I was angry with them, and I said, 'Their hearts always turn away from me. They refuse to do what I tell them.' So in my anger I took an oath: 'They will never enter my place of rest.'" Be careful then, dear brothers and sisters. Make sure that your own hearts are not evil and unbelieving, turning you away from the living God (Hebrews 3:7-12 NLT).

You must warn each other daily so that no one is deceived by sin and hardened against God. If we are faithful to the end, trusting God just as firmly as when we first believed, we will share in all that belongs to Christ. But we must never forget this warning we have been given—*today you must listen to and obey His voice.*

Words Matter

Who rebelled against God even though they had heard His voice? Were they not the ones Moses led out of the bondage of Egypt who made God angry for forty years? Was it not His people who sinned whose bodies fell in the wilderness? To whom was God speaking when He vowed they would never enter the place of rest? He was speaking to the disobedient. They were not allowed to enter into rest because of their unbelief. Evil decrees, negative proclamations, words of doubt, and unbelief provoked the angels. Don't let them also *mar* your life! They can cancel destiny promises. Promises intended for us can be withheld as we keep wandering in a wilderness of confused unbelief.

In Genesis 19, two angels were sent to help Lot and his family escape the destruction of Sodom and Gomorrah. These cities were under intense judgment because of their wickedness. The sin of homosexuality ran rampant, among other sins, and the cities were ultimately destroyed by fire and brimstone raining down from heaven (probably due to volcanic eruption). Abraham had interceded for his nephew Lot and his family who lived there, and the angel of the Lord led them out safely, commanding them as they fled to refrain from looking back. But Genesis 19:26 says that Lot's wife *did* look back, and when she did she provoked the angel of the Lord. He was not forgiving, and she was immediately turned into a pillar of salt. We must keep our eyes fixed forward. *Not heeding angelic instruction can be dangerous, and it can mar your life.*

An Angel Smote King Herod

Acts 12 shares the story of King Herod and an angel.

And Herod was highly displeased with them of Tyre and Sidon: but they came with one accord to him, and, having made Blastus the king's chamberlain their friend, desired peace; because their country was nourished by the king's country. And upon a set day Herod, arrayed in royal apparel, sat upon his throne, and made an oration unto them. And the people gave a shout, saying, It is the voice of a god, and not of a man. And immediately the angel of the Lord smote him, because he gave not God the glory: and he was eaten of worms, and gave up the ghost (Acts 12:20-23).

When Herod accepted the praise and glory as though he was God, an angel saw it and smote him with worms until he died. Perhaps it reminded this angel of Lucifer when he rebelled in heaven, taking glory that didn't belong to him. Without question, Herod provoked and chafed a watching angel. Normally, the angelic hosts are nurturing and assisting, but here we see that arrogant rebellion will sometimes cause them to react. Herod's attitude angered a heavenly warrior's sense of being.

Zacharias Provoked Gabriel

Luke 1 recounts the story of Zacharias and Elisabeth. Zacharias was a Jewish priest serving God in the temple. He and his wife Elisabeth were old and barren. They desperately wanted to have children and had prayed for such for years. One day, as Zacharias was burning incense in the sanctuary, an angel appeared to him.

> *And when Zacharias saw him, he was troubled, and fear fell upon him. But the angel said unto him, Fear not, Zacharias: for thy prayer is heard; and thy wife Elisabeth shall bear thee a son, and thou shalt call his name John. And thou shalt have joy and gladness; and many shall rejoice at his birth* (Luke 1:12-14).

You would think that Zacharias would have been ecstatic, jumping, and dancing. Finally, God had answered their prayer! Instead, Zacharias began to question the angel about what was said, provoking him:

> *And the angel answering said unto him, I am Gabriel, that stand in the presence of God; and am sent to speak unto thee, and to shew thee these glad tidings. And, behold, thou shalt be dumb, and not able to speak, until the day that these things shall be performed, because thou believest not my words, which shall be fulfilled in their season* (Luke 1:19-20).

Zacharias was immediately stricken mute and remained unable to speak until John was born.

Gabriel was on an assignment from the Godhead. It was time for Messiah to be born, and Gabriel was the angel assigned to facilitate Christ's incarnation upon the earth. He was over it all from Mary to the shepherds on the hillside. He had a lot to do! He did not have time for Zacharias' unbelief. Zacharias' unbelief chafed Gabriel, so he "hit the mute button." There was no time for games; Jesus was coming!

It is better to say nothing than to speak unbelief and provoke angels assigned to bring about God's promises in your life. It is better to say nothing than to complain and be negative. Gabriel knew that unless he could stop Zacharias from speaking doubt and unbelief the objective would not come to pass. John would have to come through someone else. Therefore, Zacharias was muted for nine months. Gabriel knew the power of a person's words. He knew the power that man's words carried. So he acted in order to prevent Zacharias' words of doubt from interfering with God's plan. *We must get a revelation of how important our actions and our words are where angels and the promises of God are concerned.*

Words of Faith

Angels are a divine warrior force behind the heirs of salvation, but they are not passive, naïve, unthinking beings who minister regardless of what we do. We cannot live any way we want to and have God's Kingdom behind us. We cannot live undisciplined, uncommitted lives and have the assistance of angelic hosts. We must understand that we are destined to live the life we speak. Angels know it; demons know it; but many people today do not understand it.

Why is the church not influencing the world as it should? Why are Christians not reaching the harvest for souls about which Joel prophesied? Why are there so few miracles? Why the empty unfulfilled promises? Angels may have been provoked.

Our actions and our words can "ground" our Heir Force. God would not have warned us not to provoke them if it were not greatly important. Everything He says is for a reason. Impotent, lifeless words cause angels to be discontent. We *mar* our lives with evil decrees or words.

God's Word is true. We should not retreat from standing with it. Rebellion to God's sexual laws is being winked at under the guise of politically correct thinking. Homosexuality occurs, due to a silent church's passivity. Adultery, pornography, lusts of the flesh, greed, broken covenant, apathy, lying, conniving, and backbiting cause barrenness of soul and bitter tears. They make the angels discontent. The murmuring, complaining, and griping of the saints provokes and grieves angels, grounding the Heir Force.

We constantly hear believers—and even pastors!—say that we are never going to reach all the world in these awful times. *Miracles were for Bible days. The church is going under. This or that portion of Scripture is really not relevant any longer. People today are just too hard to reach for Christ. There are a lot of gods out there. This world system is just too ingrained into people, and we will never be able to get it out. We will never be able to overcome that sin or bondage. The coming generation is too wrapped up in sin to ever change. I feel hopeless about it. Why even try? Why even come into the church office this week? Why try anything? I feel powerless and overwhelmed.* I wonder if the angels ever say, "If we could just get the saints to hush, we could get on with God's plan. If we could just get them to stop talking unbelief, if we could ever just get them to stop quoting demons, we could get something done."

It is time for a new generation of saints, new in attitude and lifestyle. It is time for a divine shift into true Christianity with the decision made to quit playing as if we are *going* to do it and for us to simply *do it*. It is time to quit pretending. It is time to conduct ourselves as believers who release the Heir Force and loose the Kingdom. It is time for the faith-decreeing church to arise. It is time to align our words boldly and unashamedly with God's Word. It is time to decree God's will on earth, done in Jesus' name. It is time to launch the Heir Force. It is time to launch a new move of God in America. It is time to stop marring the remnant church. It is time to stop marring our lives and our families, and to stop chafing angels with our negative words.

We need to empower the angel network and the Kingdom of Heaven by decreeing words of faith.

Jesus is the King of Hope. He is all powerful. We should be declaring this: that God is the same yesterday, today, and forever. Miracles are for today. The church is getting stronger and more relevant. It is prosperous. Its influence is growing. We need to decree that people are hungry for God. They want to know Him. We need to decree that the Creator is never outdated. This world's systems and all its technologies are made for now, made for us to preach Jesus as never before. What opportunities are before us! There has never been more darkness, so our light will shine brighter! The coming generation is hungry for God, and they are coming to Jesus by the millions because He has what they truly desire. They will prophesy. They will see signs, wonders, and miracles. They will move in God's power. Harvest is coming to this nation by the millions! Success is inevitable because no weapon formed against us can prosper, and if God be for us who can successfully be against us?

Our great God has promised, "I will be an enemy to your enemy and an adversary to your adversary. I'll be on your side. My angels will go before you and lead you into My promises. Live in such a way that you construct an atmosphere for My Kingdom advancement. *Do not provoke My angels. Do not ground them. Launch them! Release them with words of faith!*"

ANGELS AND
PRAYER DECREES

Thou shalt also decree a thing, and it shall be established unto thee: and the light shall shine upon thy ways (Job 22:28).

You shall also decide and decree a thing, and it shall be established for you; and the light [of God's favor] shall shine upon your ways (Job 22:28 AMP).

The word *thing* in the above verse is the Hebrew word *omer*, meaning "a word or a promise" (Strong, H562). The heirs of God and the joint heirs with Christ have authority to decree words of Scripture, words of promise, words of prophecy (which are also words of God given through Holy Spirit enlightenment). Those words, in Jesus' name, will be established. *Established* is the Hebrew word *quwm*, meaning "to be made good, to perform, succeed, to raise up and come to be or to pass" (Strong, H6965). *Quwm* is used in the Hebrew language as a construction word. When you decree a word, you are constructing it into your life. You're building it to appear on your life's pathway. It becomes performed into your life's ways; it's why words are so important. When we decree a word of the Lord, when we speak a promise, when we speak a principle or a prophecy that is based upon God's Word, His favor anoints that word to come to pass in our lives.

The word *way* is the Hebrew word *derek,* meaning "a road or a path" (Strong, H1870). It refers to the course of life, life's journey, or a way of life. When we speak a word that is based upon what God says, it's made good on our life's journey. It comes into our path and intersects our life at some point. It also rouses angel armies to assist us. Remember, Psalm 103:20 says that angels listen for God's Word that we speak. Why? To bring those words or promises to pass, to intersect them with our life and cause them to be constructed and built into our life's journey. When we speak our faith, when we say what God says, angels hearken to it and organize to make it good. They assist the heirs, the born-again ones, by helping it come to pass. Angels help construct and connect us to its fulfillment.

Decrees are like prophecy. When you decree a word, you are prophesying into the course of your life. You are prophesying your future. Angels will hearken to bring it to pass. It is vital that we pray what God says. It is vital that we declare our faith, speaking His words over our lives. Hearkening angels will begin building them into our future.

To close this book, I felt I should put the principles I've written about into decrees. It is more than a review; it is an important key that releases angels. Every decree that follows is based upon the Word of God and is taught in the previous chapters. I encourage you to stir your faith and speak these decrees out loud over your life. Doing so will loose angels sent to assist you.

"I" or "We" Decree:

1. The greatest days in church history are not in our past; they are in our present and our future.

2. Holy Spirit is now supervising a new movement of awesome revival.

3. Angel Armies are ascending and descending. We are under an open heaven.

4. Angels are ministering fresh fire from heaven's altar (it's purging iniquity off of us).

5. Power from heaven is flowing to us and through us.

6. Holy Spirit is breathing life into our King's campaign.

7. Holy Spirit is breathing life into miracles, healings, and wonders in the heavens and on the earth.

8. A movement that moves is now moving.

9. Holy Spirit is coming to us now with far more of the angels than He did on Pentecost in Acts 2.

10. Angel Armies are being commissioned to be present and minister to us and with us.

11. Angel activity is increasing exponentially.

12. Revival greater than Pentecost in Acts 2 is now flowing to us and through us.

13. Greater power than has ever been seen in church history is now flowing to us and through us.

14. There is now an alignment of heaven's Angel Army with the Remnant Warrior army and the War Eagle army of the coming generation.

15. They will now synergize together under Holy Spirit supervision to demonstrate that the Kingdom of God is present, energized, activated, and successful.

16. Power for mighty deliverance—be loosed.

17. Power for Kingdom exploits—be loosed.

18. Deep currents of Holy Spirit power that produce the largest harvest of souls in history—be loosed.

19. Angel Network—be loosed to help gather harvest.

20. New strategies of evangelism—be loosed.

21. Revelation and enlightenment—be loosed.

22. We loose the Heir Force (the assisters of the heirs of Christ).

23. We loose Angel Armies.

24. We loose the troops of heaven to fight alongside of us.

25. In Jesus' name, we deploy them.

26. Activate the campaign of King Jesus and Holy Spirit in this nation.

27. Angels carrying and assisting the King's anointing—be loosed.

28. Angels assisting the Holy Spirit and fresh outpourings—be loosed.

29. God-activity, that only God's ability can create—be loosed among us.

30. Holy Spirit, execute God activity right here and right now.

31. Release God happenings in the church.

32. We will participate in God happenings.

33. We will see more angel activity than demon activity. We forbid demon activity in Jesus' name.

34. We have far more righteous angels on our side than demons against us. The natural number is not the Kingdom number.

35. Lord Sabbaoth, the Lord of Angel Armies, is on our side. We will win!

36. In Jesus' name, enemy resistance in the natural realms or spiritual realms is being scattered and shattered.

37. Angels are striking the enemies of the King.

38. Angels are ambushing hell's forces as our praise ascends.

39. Our praise decrees are producing victory that looks impossible.

40. The Kingdom of God is now being extended locally, regionally, and throughout the earth.

41. Bold, passionate, energized, and authoritative angels are assisting us to do the works of Jesus.

42. The Angel Armies are camped all around us because we respect the Lord and decree His Word.

43. In Jesus' name, we loose them now. Work for us. Assist us.

44. Angels are circling to protect our borders.

45. Angels are revolving around us to deliver and bring salvation in the spirit realms and natural realms.

46. Angels are present-time deliverers here, right now, to deliver us.

47. Angels are circling to make ugly situations turn to lovely.

48. In Jesus' name, be loosed to take hold of bad circumstances and events on life's journey and turn them around for our good.

49. We loose angels to rescue, strip away bondages, remove obstacles that hinder, and protect us from hell's strategies.

50. We loose angels to lead us to unbelievers who are receptive to Jesus.

51. We loose angels to bring us messages in dreams.

52. Dreams, be loosed to provide guidance in Jesus' name.

53. We loose angels who bring answers to prayers, just like Daniel and Revelation describe.

54. Angels who organize around the prayers of the saints and help bring them to pass are working now in our lives.

55. Angels who organize around our prayers for this region (as Holy Spirit supervises) assist us in doing the work of the ministry.

56. We ask You, Lord Jesus, to release Angel Armies to bring answers to our prayers.

57. Release angels to tip the prayer bowls of heaven into the fire on Your altar.

58. We decree heaven's Angel Armies are released into the affairs of men as a result of our crying out to You, O God.

59. We cry out, God, give us mercy. Grant us loving-kindness. Hear our prayers.

60. We invite, in Jesus' name, angels to come execute judgment upon deep-rooted iniquity in our region and nation.

61. Engage in combat against sin and perversion.

62. Engage with us and fight doctrines of devils.

63. Angels who go before us to open doors—be loosed in Jesus' name.

64. Angels who go ahead to prepare our way for success—be loosed in Jesus' name.

65. Angels who cut off enemy attacks—be loosed in Jesus' name.

66. Angels who arrange divine connections to people or events—be loosed in Jesus' name.

67. Angels who assist prophetic promises to come to pass—be loosed in Jesus' name. Bring them to us; accelerate them.

68. Angels who bring messages from the Godhead—be loosed in Jesus' name.

69. Holy Spirit, release the angels who bring enlightenment and revelation.

70. Angels who bring us supernatural strength to finish our assignments—be released in Jesus' name.

71. Release the angels of strength.

72. Strengthen us to overcome and reign with Jesus.

73. Release, in this region, angels who attack Jezebels, Absaloms, and Ahabs.

74. Loose them to free our assignments.

75. Loose them to give us great victory.

76. Loose them to protect us from property being stolen from us.

77. Send the angels who strengthen Your church and Your people.

78. We loose strength to stand and win.

79. We are strong in the Lord and in the power of His might.

80. We declare the Kingdom of God grows and prevails.

81. We decree the zeal of the Lord of Hosts will perform it.

82. The Lord says, "It is time for a new release of My Holy Spirit power. The King's anointing and authority will increase in unprecedented, delegated proportions. The Angel Network is assisting Holy Spirit in exalting heaven's King, and now the young and the old will participate in the greatest movement of My Kingdom in history!"

83. The trans-generational outpouring prophesied by Joel—be loosed upon us now in Jesus' name.

84. Anointing on all flesh—be loosed to us and through us.

85. Anointing for increased dreams and visions—be released to us.

86. Lost harvests will now be restored to us.

87. Lost property will now be restored to us.

88. Lost finances will now be restored to us.

89. Lost business will now be restored to us.

90. The years the locusts, the palmer worms, and the canker worms have eaten will now be restored.

91. Multitudes (millions) in the valley of decision will be saved.

92. Our great God has sworn this to us in an oath of obligation and angels are hearkening to it to bring it to pass.

93. We decree angels who assist kingdoms to shift their regions into alignment with God's will—be loosed.

94. Angels who help apostles shift their regions—be loosed now in Jesus' name.

95. Angels who partner with apostolic assignments—be released now in Jesus' name.

96. Sent ones, come to us and do the head of the church's bidding. We welcome your ministry.

97. Come and help us extend His Kingdom throughout this nation.

98. Angels, help us complete Kingdom business in this nation.

99. Angels who bring great deliverance to apostles—be released now in Jesus' name.

100. We decree confinement be broken and great liberty be restored.

101. Liberty to do their apostolic assignments—be loosed.

102. In Jesus' name, we forbid hell's hindrance to their assignments to work.

103. Release warriors from heaven to partner with apostolic vision.

104. Release angels to assist in shifting Your Kingdom in this nation into harvest mode.

105. We decree a shift from bondage to liberty—be loosed.

106. A shift from being owned to owning—be loosed.

107. Power for new beginnings—be loosed.

108. Power to be fruitful and multiply—be loosed.

109. Gifts of Holy Spirit—be loosed in greater measure than ever before.

110. Words of wisdom—be loosed.

111. Words of knowledge—be loosed.

112. Gift of faith—be loosed.

113. Gift of healings—be loosed.

114. Workings of miracles—be loosed.

115. Prophecy—be loosed.

116. Discerning of spirits—be loosed.

117. Tongues and interpretation—be loosed.

118. In Jesus' name, we ask for the gifts of Holy Spirit to move among us.

119. We decree we will move with the Holy Spirit.

120. We will move forward.

121. We decree a shift in this nation to move from complacency to discipleship. From intimidation to valor. From hopelessness to confidence. From four walls inside buildings to the streets. From selfish Christianity to servant Christianity. From consumer Christianity to discipleship. From lost harvest to ingathering.

122. We decree that resources are being restored and multiplied.

123. We decree the generations are rowing together and Angel Armies are assisting Holy Spirit's campaign to bring in the greatest harvest of souls that has ever been seen.

124. We ask Holy Spirit to loose harvest right here and right now.

125. We decree we are entering into a new season.

126. We are leaving the dock. Our sails are up, gathering Holy Spirit breezes. We are sailing into deep waters.

127. New things never done before will now be done.

128. New strategies, blessed by Holy Spirit, will now be done, assisted by Angel Armies in Jesus' name.

129. Holy Spirit is now implementing a major shift in the Kingdom of God in this entire region and in this nation.

130. He is now releasing the revival of King Jesus. It is the last days outpouring. It is the greatest ingathering of harvest the world has ever seen.

131. The angels of heaven are now activated and released under Holy Spirit supervision to accelerate the shift into harvest mode and to assist the reaping.

132. In Jesus' name, we loose angels to assist us in gathering harvest.

133. Harvest angels, be released now to accomplish our King's commission with us.

134. We decree—harvest multiply. Multiply now at levels never seen before.

135. Angels, help us target millions in the valley of decision.

136. We loose the convicting power of the Holy Spirit to draw multitudes to repentance.

137. We loose the Gospel, which is the power of God, to be fruitful and multiply.

138. We decree our faith—delay no longer.

139. Angels sent to deal with delay—be loosed in Jesus' name.

140. We forbid delay. We forbid hindering demon spirits. We bind their work in Jesus' name.

141. Holy Spirit, release Angel Armies against hindering spirits and delays.

142. Come, Holy Spirit. Empower the Gospel of the Kingdom in tangible ways. Let Your power be seen.

143. Come, Angel Armies, and open doors for the Gospel of truth to prevail.

144. Angels who are sent to facilitate the Gospel of salvation through Jesus—be loosed.

145. Angels sent to assist us to scatter and shatter all demon influenced blockades—be loosed in Jesus' name.

146. We decree in Jesus' name, all doors, channels, paths, roads, highways, and byways—be opened before us.

147. Angels anointed to bring great awakening—be loosed in Jesus' name.

148. Assist us under Holy Spirit power to awaken Christ's church, awaken the passive, awaken the cold believers, awaken the lukewarm, awaken the lethargic in faith.

149. Angels help us awaken the hearts of dispassionate, part-time Christians who have embraced hell's delusional compromise.

150. Shake them from their slumber. Challenge the iniquity of their heart. Bring heaven's fire.

151. Holy Spirit, bring angels as tongues of fire, like the day of Pentecost, to confront dispassionate Christianity.

152. We ask You, Lord, loose Holy Spirit's fire among us. Loose it today. Loose it here.

153. Release holy angels of fire among us to burn iniquity from the hearts, the minds, and the lips of believers in this region.

154. Send Your fire. Let it blaze.

155. Send awakening fire.

156. Fire of God, fall on us like the day of Pentecost in Acts 2.

157. We decree Holy Spirit and angels of fire are welcome among us as our King ordains.

158. We decree we are shifting from oppression to glory.

159. God's glorious presence will be visibly seen in this nation.

160. We ask that the awesome, weighty presence of God become heavier and heavier.

161. We ask that Your glory be as a thick cloud and pillars of fire.

162. We invite Your holy presence. Come be God among us. Manifest Your glory. Reveal Your glory in this region. Reveal Your glory to us and through us in this nation.

163. We have prepared an upper room over our lives, our families, and this region. Come fill that upper room with Your glory.

164. Pour out Your Spirit in this upper room right here and now.

165. We loose Angel Armies who ride the rays of Your presence.

166. We decree the New Testament church will now emerge from the culture to rule and reign with Christ.

167. We decree we will be filled and refilled with the Holy Spirit and power from heaven.

168. We decree that God's heaven, Holy Spirit, and His angels, in partnership with the New Testament church, will now work together in the greatest mission of the church in all of time. The young and the old will participate together.

169. The Third Great Awakening of King Jesus has begun in this nation and this region and will now accelerate.

170. A new Jesus movement is beginning to move, greater than the charismatic movement. This one will be a Jesus movement on steroids.

171. Loose the Angel Armies sent to assist a new Jesus movement.

172. We agree with You, Lord. We agree with Your words. We agree with Your will. Revival roll through America.

173. We hear the marching troops of heaven. We hear the sound of revival, awakening, and reformation. In Jesus' name we march to see it done.

174. We embrace the call of heaven to move and retake the land.

175. Angels who do God's good pleasure in our lives—be loosed in Jesus' name.

176. Strong, watchful, listening beings of wisdom and power, circle us right now to minister the good will of God in concrete, real ways.

177. Angels who cause the benefits of the Kingdom of Christ to materialize for us—be loosed in Jesus' name.

178. Angels who cause the benefits to stick to us like honey on our hands—be loosed.

179. We decree the sticky favor of God is all over Christ's heirs.

180. Long lasting benefits are materializing for our families. They are intersecting with our families' life journeys.

181. Angels are surrounding us to bring it to pass.

182. In Jesus' name, we release angels who assist the release of the high priestly anointing of Jesus to us and through us. It's a breakthrough anointing.

183. Angels who cause justice of freedom to intersect with our lives—be loosed.

184. Angels who cause God's promises to materialize—be loosed.

185. We free all God's promises to happen in our lives. Intersect with us.

186. We free all of our rights as heirs of God to come to us.

187. Angels who are bringers of Kingdom blessings—be loosed.

188. Angels who are sent to assist our destiny—be loosed in Jesus' name.

189. Angels sent to reveal and draw out our God-given purpose, our God-given potential—be loosed in Jesus' name.

190. Angels who connect us to people, places, circumstances, events, and to our purpose—be loosed in Jesus' name.

191. Angels who assist Holy Spirit in leading God's plan for our lives before we were ever born—be loosed in Jesus' name.

192. We were born for these times.

193. We declare our potential is loosed and angel assisted, in Jesus' name.

194. We declare our destiny is Holy Spirit empowered.

195. We confess, we decree, we speak forth from our nature to believe—I will fulfill my purpose. I will complete my destiny. I will reach to more and more of my potential.

196. The gifts, talents, and abilities God put in me are being anointed to reach new levels.

197. Angels assigned to me the day I was born have been briefed concerning my purpose, and they are partnering with me to accomplish God's will for my life.

198. God has placed a future and a hope before me and it's all good.

199. He who has begun a good work in me will complete it.

200. Angels are present-time ministers connecting me to destiny assignments. They are protecting my purpose. They are wrestling destiny out of me.

201. Angels sent to bring us success, prosperity, and financial security—be loosed in Jesus' name.

202. Angels who connect us to places, people, events, business, material properties, sales, jobs, and job promotions that prosper us—be loosed in Jesus' name.

203. Angels assigned to intersect our lives with financial blessings—be loosed in Jesus' name.

204. Angels who watch our offerings and minister covenant rights to Christ's heirs—be loosed in Jesus' name.

205. The tithe brought to God's house causes Jehovah Jireh (our Provider) to open the heavens over our lives and families.

206. Angels ascend and descend through that open heaven, bringing providential blessings.

207. Angels orbiting our lives, descending from paths opened in the heavenly places to give us financial breakthroughs, be loosed in Jesus' name.

208. Angels from pathways in the skies are working to transfer the wealth of the wicked to Christ's heirs. Be loosed in Jesus' name.

209. We decree wealth is being transferred to us individually and corporately.

210. Angels descending from the breaker Himself (Jesus) are carrying His breaker anointing to intersect with our lives.

211. They are coming to bust up financial bondage.

212. They are coming to supernaturally remove debt.

213. They are scattering and shattering whatever devours the finances of the saints.

214. Under the divine oversight of Father God, angels assigned to us are fighting off the devourer that our God has rebuked.

215. Angels are assisting the Godhead's release of blessings (spiritually, physically, and materially) upon our homes and extended family.

216. In Jesus' name, we release them to ascend and descend.

217. Angels sent to show us rams caught in the thicket (provision we knew nothing about)—be loosed in Jesus' name.

218. Angels sent to reveal hidden treasure we knew nothing about—be loosed in Jesus' name.

219. Angels, lead us to places of great resources that God has prepared for us.

220. The same God who opened a Promised Land for Moses and Israel is doing it for us. Places of promise are opening to us.

221. In Jesus' name, we loose angels sent to lead us to places of great resources.

222. We decree that people we don't even know are being used by Holy Spirit and His angels to bless us. Angels are intersecting them with our lives.

223. Angels sent to lead us into inheritance we knew nothing about—be loosed in Jesus' name.

224. We decree abundance, prosperity, plenty—be released.

225. Covenant blessings of financial success—be released now in Jesus' name.

226. Devourer, you're rebuked by God off the lives of every covenant heir, just like God says.

227. We declare freedom.

228. The windows of heaven are open over us, just like God's Word says.

229. Blessings are coming upon us and overtaking us.

230. Bonuses are coming upon us.

231. Checks in the mail we knew nothing about are coming.

232. Deals, great deals, are coming upon Your heirs, O God.

233. Inheritance is finding us.

234. Stocks and bonds are blessed and blessed and blessed.

235. Property value will accelerate in worth.

236. We decree the wealth of the sinner is being laid up for us, just as Your Word says.

237. Prosperity, be released now.

238. In Jesus' name, we bind lack and loose abundance.

239. We bind poverty and loose plenty.

240. We bind neediness and loose finances.

241. We bind poor living and loose success.

242. You have ordained us to bear much fruit.

243. We decree we are a fruitful people.

244. We are blessed in the city and we are blessed in the country.

245. We're blessed coming in and going out.

246. The Lord commands His blessings upon us, just as Deuteronomy 28 says.

247. God blesses the works of our hands.

248. He makes us plenteous in goods.

249. He opens His good treasure over us and rains it down upon us.

250. Angels sent to connect us to covenant prosperity—be loosed in Jesus' name.

251. Angels sent to assist Christ's church to extend His Kingdom into this nation—be loosed in Jesus' name.

252. We are here to establish the rule of God's Word, His statutes, His covenants, His laws, and His principles, and King Jesus is releasing Angel Armies to help us do it.

253. Holy Spirit is empowering it from heaven through the greatest outpouring of the Holy Spirit that has ever occurred.

254. Waves of Holy Spirit enablement are now gathering Angel Armies to partner with the church to battle for the throne of their region.

255. Holy Spirit empowerment, strategies, and Angel Armies will assist the New Testament church to bind hell's tactics and loose the Gospel of the Kingdom.

256. The church will govern regions, decreeing what God says.

257. We rise now to occupy the throne of our region.

258. King Jesus gives us authority to overrule hell's government. We make that ruling today and Angel Armies are now assisting us.

259. We rise to make ruling decrees backed by Father God, King Jesus, Holy Spirit, the Kingdom of Heaven, and Angel Armies.

260. In Jesus' name, we cleanse the heavens over our region of principalities and powers of darkness.

261. We cast down and displace demon princes from iniquitous thrones. Be removed in Jesus' name.

262. Your rights to this territory are broken by superior power and authority. It was broken by the cross and the blood of Jesus.

263. The New Testament church overrules the kingdom of hell, in Jesus' name.

264. The power of God destroys your strongholds, in Jesus' name.

265. Holy Spirit and His angels are working with the New Testament church to take the seat of power in this region.

266. The heirs, seated with Christ in heavenly places, occupy the territorial thrones of this region.

267. We will occupy seats of power and influence for Christ's Kingdom.

268. Angels are protecting us, delivering us, and enforcing our decrees of faith.

269. Powers, mights, and dominions of hell will be shaken down from their positions of influence.

270. Our God is right now shaking the earth and the heavens.

271. Jesus, loose Angel Armies to battle against fallen demons. Battle them with us.

272. Loose battalions of angels ordained for these times on earth.

273. We decree hell's ideology, oppressive nature, lust for power, idolatry, greed, and demon thinking promoted through rebel government—be bound in Jesus' name.

274. Angels sent to assist us in overruling rebel government—be loosed in Jesus' name.

275. Angels sent to assist us in removing oppressive government—be loosed in Jesus' name.

276. God, call rebel powers of the sky and rebel kings in on the carpet.

277. God, we ask You to punish the hosts of hell and the rebel kings who oppress us.

278. In Jesus' name, we (the heirs, the *ekklesia*, the church) overthrow demon powers in this region and nation.

279. We sit with Christ, occupying the spiritual throne of rule as commanded in the dominion mandate.

280. We will affect the function and release of natural government upon the earth for our King Jesus.

281. Righteousness will prevail. Our King will be honored. The Word of the Lord will be obeyed.

282. The true New Testament church of Jesus will rise to change rebel government and disciple this nation.

283. God is not done with America. The covenants made with our founding fathers will prevail.

284. America will be ablaze with revival.

285. America will see the greatest awakening in history.

286. We will not be silent cowards.

287. We will not be cowardly, submissive, spineless, politically correct appeasers.

288. We will not compromise the truth.

289. We will say what God says.

290. We will say it boldly, with passion, and do so every single time.

291. We will prophesy the Word of the Lord.

292. Our definition of right and wrong will not be blurred by experimental doctrines of demons.

293. We are those who stand for God's ways, fixed and unmovable.

294. God's Word of truth will be our testimony.

295. The stars from their orbits, the angels from their orbits, are fighting alongside of us.

296. Angels from their spheres are fighting principalities and powers according to our decrees.

297. Angels are orbiting to hearken to God's Word that we decree.

298. They are hearkening to prophetic words that we decree.

299. They are listening for prayers we pray in alignment with God's will.

300. They are moving with power to bring God's Word to pass.

301. They are moving with power to give us great victories.

302. They are moving from their heavenly spheres, empowered by Holy Spirit, to give supernatural breakthroughs to God's people.

303. We, the remnant church, will declare what God says. Angels will hear it and together we will fight hell and win.

Amen

.

Appendix:
Prophecies of
Confirmation

Prophecy #1: Realignment, Empowerment, and Joy— Chuck Pierce (November, 2010)

For the Lord said, "Even now as Ohio turns, you will turn twelve regions in the U.S. I say this is a day of promotion. Let your nerve structures come into a new alignment, for I will be joining people with you to empower you with joy. You will be filled with such joy. Doors will open that could not open before. I will move you from this nation to twelve nations. There is a release and a new word forming in your mouth. From this word, governments will realign."

This word was given prior to the eighty days of prayer and worship my congregation took part in. After this word from the Lord was given, the prophet thanked the Lord for the multiple meetings that would be filled with worshipers. He said, "The rafters will ring. The Lord says, 'It is going to be so filled with worship, it will be louder than any sports activity in Cleveland or Cincinnati. The rafters of this place will ring in days ahead. It will be a ring of worship that changes the course of this nation.'"

PROPHECY #2: TIME TO ALIGN— ANNE TATE (NOVEMBER, 2010)

The Lord says, "In this season, I will send Lord Sabaoth suddenly to a gathering. When He arrives, you will have a moment to decide if you are going to align with Him or not. As you make that choice to align with Him, you will so agree with the Armies of the Host of God that He is able to amass and align the armies of the host of earth. This is the season that must come forth, because My pulpit was always called to compete with, pull down, and challenge the thrones of iniquity that abide in a territory. My people and the power of My pulpit have not always gone forth. In order to enter the kingdom battle of this season, I am calling you to what will make a difference on the earth. There will have to be a new alignment with Lord Sabaoth. As you align, I will release the angelic into new and greater dimensions as you stand in place with Me. You have been chosen for this purpose. As the body of Christ aligns, the rest of the nation will begin to shift and align with Armies of the Host of Heaven. I care not if it is only the 300 of Gideon. It will be enough. You stand and when He appears you shall be like Him."

PROPHECY #3: THE HEARTBEAT— JANE HAMON (AUGUST, 2010)

The Lord says, "I want you to know that I have assigned specific angels to work and walk with you. I want you to know that I am going to release My 'big guns' to you. There are going to be times when Michael comes and works with you. There are going to be other times when Gabriel comes and talks to you. There has already been some revelation I released to you that you have not understood. When the angel Gabriel came to Daniel, he brought understanding of things too hard for Daniel to comprehend. I am going to send My angel Gabriel and he is going to bring that understanding to you, so you can move forward into this next season. I am going to cause a new supernatural alignment to begin in this state. Some of the most unsuspecting leaders are going to link up with you, because they have the vision. They are going to come out of denominational churches. They are going come out of some old-line places, too. The embers of awakening have already started in them. They are going to blow. You are going to blow by the breath of the Spirit. You are going to release that breath and begin to stir those embers to full flame. This is a time that I have you focused in this state. Son and Daughter, understand the reason—for that is the heart of the nation. As you breathe life into this heart, you are going to find that the whole nation begins to come alive and begins to pound and pulse with the heartbeat of heaven. You have been telling My heart to beat again by focusing on your state. You are whispering in the ear of your state and you are saying, 'You need to tell your heart to beat again, because the heartbeat has not started.' As you tell your state to beat again, you are going to see the entire nation begin to rise up and come alive to the purposes of God."

This word is interesting because of an Ohio bill nicknamed "The Heartbeat Bill," which says you cannot perform abortion once the heartbeat of the baby has begun. The heartbeat of a baby has been proven to begin beating as young as eighteen days old. This bill would literally save hundreds of thousands of lives. The prophetess who gave this prophetic word certainly did not know anything about this bill before she gave this word, yet it was so strategic and specific that discerning it to be a word against abortion is essential. Because Ohio is presenting this bill, there are representatives coming from all over wanting to know how they can get that bill introduced in their state. Ohio is rewriting the evil decrees in the name of Jesus.

Another word came forth around the same time as the one I just mentioned. The man who gave this word said he literally saw the

State of Ohio with arteries and blood flowing in them. There have been multiple confirmations about this.

Prophecy #4: Torchbearing and Delegation— Bishop Bill Hamon (November, 2007)

This word to my church goes back to 2007, but I think it is certainly relevant and a confirmation to some of the things the body of Christ has been seeing.

The Lord said, "I am going to use you as key players to begin to shift some things. You just keep carrying My people into My presence. You keep carrying My people even into My purpose. You keep carrying My people into the anointing and you will see the anointing truly break the yoke. It truly does destroy the yoke of the enemy. There will be a fire that will go from person to person, from place to place, and it is going to be launched out of here. I see people coming from the surrounding area to dip the torch in the fire that is being lit in this place. I have made you My torchbearers of truth, of My presence, and of My purpose. Now, Son and Daughter, understand that this is to be a day of rising up and also of delegation, because I am not asking you to do all and be all. There will be some things, trans-locally involved in, that are going to take your time, effort, and energy away from the local house. That is strategically planned by Me, and I want you to know that I am putting people in place who are trustworthy and can shoulder the burden to carry the responsibility. Things will shift and transition a bit, but I am not loosing you from this house. There will be other things that I am going to have you do apostolically in this new season. Get ready. Put your running shoes on, because the pace is accelerating, and in the mist of acceleration there is going to come multiplication. The enemy thought he would sift you. The enemy thought he would shift you like Gideon's revival last year. I want you to know that I was in the sifting. I was in the shifting, and now you have your Gideon's three hundred. Now watch and see the acceleration bring the multiplication to cause Kingdom purposes to be established in this place."

Over six hundred churches have dipped their torch in the fire through my church in Ohio. Do you realize what a miracle it is to get over six hundred churches to work together?

PROPHECY #5: NEW STRENGTH— CINDY JACOBS (JANUARY, 2010)

The Lord says, "I am causing Ohio to be a state of generals who will put the rest of the nation in order. Many of you have been in great battles and you are weary," but the Lord says, "today, receive strength."

PROPHECY #6: STANDING BOLDLY— TIM SHEETS (FEBRUARY, 2011)

The Lord says, "I have lions hidden in My remnant, not wolves. They will now arise to patrol and remove the defeated ones—the wolf packs that have come to scatter My flocks. My lions will not be intimidated, but will be fierce, bold, and aggressive. A new roar will be heard from My tribe, announcing territorial dominion. A roar claiming geographical and spiritual jurisdiction shall sound from My remnant. A roar of rule against hell's power shall be sounded. A roar of authority in My Name shall come against hell's intruders. My called ones shall now step forth and move in My power. They will manifest their rights as sons and daughters ruling and reigning with Me, as intended. They shall now display disdain for enemy princes, for their might, and for the rulers of darkness, no longer compromising in shared rule, cohabitation, or shared occupancy. Loathsome passive agreement will now become a backbone of steel, upset and on fire from My holy ingots, now the voice and shout of the King! Determined faith shall now been seen in My faithful ones as they march to remove spirits from the land. No shared rule. My rule, which shall prevail for My warriors. Power to prevail is being poured out—power to overcome hell's strategies. Power to more than conquer demon tactics is being released. Those who stand with Me shall see hell's fire misfire. So arise and rule and roar with My authority. I will fill your enemies' mouths with sand and their hearts with quicksand. They will find themselves stuck in their own mire. Roar with my freedom. Roar with my liberty. Let rejoicing roar out of Zion. March into battle with confident peace. Great peace and revival fire shall now begin to burn through Ohio as My Third Great Awakening begins to roll. Indeed the region will become activated by My glory. My shaking has come. Walls, strongholds, obstacles, and hell's fortifications are being shaken down even as you are being shaken free. My shaking will open ancient wells of revival. I will shake open the ancient wells of healing, miracles, and mighty deliverance. I will shake open the capped wells of evangelism, holiness, and gifts of My Spirit. New roads, inroads, mantles of wholeness, vision, harvest. Behold, I will do new things and you shall know it. You shall see it. Now it shall spring forth because your cries have come before your God. Because you have pursued My presence and your worship has become a sweet savor, the Lord and Head of the church, Jesus, King of Kings, decrees over His remnant that they shall begin *Reality Church*: no more acting, actors, or pretending—rather *real* church, disciples, Christianity, worship, power, glory, miracles, and healing. It is ordained *Reality Church*. I am removing the arrows shot into ministers—arrows of betrayal, Jezebel, Absalom, deceit, gossip born in lying spirits, and those shot by bound religious demons. I, your God, am removing the arrows. You will be free. You will be healed. You will be restored. And you will be on fire with My presence, for I have said I will make My ministers a flame of fire. It is ordained. Your place of pain shall now be a place in which you reign. It is finished. Arise and rule with Me. I am now coming to My remnant in My *Reality Churches* as Lord Saboath, Lord of Hosts, Lord of the Angel Armies. Because of your decision to align with My purpose, I will now align My Host to assist you. There is now beginning an amassing of the Angel Armies and the church's army into a divine coalition. It is a coalition of those who are willing to run into the battle, not from it. Both My earthly and heavenly army will challenge thrones of iniquity, idolatry, rebellion, witchcraft, humanism, and antichrist dominions. Battalions are dispatched and awaiting the decree of My words through the saints. My greatest campaign on earth is due. Decree it. When you align your words with My words, angel forces will align with you. Align with the angel forces in Ohio and it will accelerate an alignment in your nation. Yes, revival is now. The harvest is now. The victory is now. Arise and pursue, arise and roar, arise and fight, arise and shine, for your Light has come and the glory of the Lord has risen upon you."

Prophecy #7: It All Begins with the Heart— Jane Hamon

The Lord said, "It all starts with the heart." Revival must begin in our own hearts before it will spread to anyone around us. The embers of our hearts must begin to burn passionately with the fire of God before it will set anyone else's heart ablaze. Yet, our own hearts are not entirely what God is referring to. In this vision, the person saw the state of Ohio begin to burn like molten lava, a deep red at first, but then hints of orange. As worship continued to take place around Ohio, the fire grew hotter and brighter, turning from red to orange and then to a bright orange-yellow in color. God said again, "It all starts with the heart." They then saw the fire in Ohio begin to spill onto surrounding states. The fire continued to spread moving like hot lava until it covered the entire nation. God said again, "It all begins with the heart."

The heart is one of the most vital organs in the body. It never rests. As long as the heart is functioning properly, the rest of the body receives blood, which is the life source of the body. If the heart is damaged and can no longer function efficiently, the rest of the body suffers and cannot function as intended. If the heart of this nation functions as we were created to, the rest of the body (the nation) will be able to function as God intends. It starts with the heart. Jeremiah 20:9 says, *"His word burns in my heart like a fire"* (NLT). Why lava? Nothing can stop lava from flowing. The only thing that will stop the flow of lava is if it is completely cut off from its source. If it remains connected to its source, it will continue to flow. Lava consumes absolutely everything in its path.

Prophecy #8: We Are Embers— Rachel Shafer

Jeremiah 20:9 says, *"His word burns in my heart like a fire. It's like a fire in my bones! I am worn out trying to hold it in! I can't do it!"* (NLT). The word *embers* kept jumping out at me. Embers are so consumed with fire and burnt so completely that they can be easily blown by the wind. Wherever an ember lands, it starts a fire. Embers are often more of a problem in a forest fire than the forest fire itself, because they cause the fire to scatter and spread quickly. I believe God is calling us to be His holy embers—those who are so thoroughly consumed and on fire for Him that we will be led by the wind of the Holy Spirit and ignite fires wherever they land. Wherever the Holy Spirit leads and plants us, we are igniting fires.

Prophecy #9: Wet Wood

The Lord is saying to me that there are some people who feel they have wet wood and, thus, do not feel like a part of the Kingdom activity happening on earth. But the wonderful thing about wet wood is that this fire is hot enough to burn through wet wood. If you have a desire to become an ember and catch the fire, you have to put your wet wood out before the Lord. This means that holding everything in is not going to catch you on fire; however, if you bring it out, bringing yourself before the Lord, He can burn through anything. He can make you an ember. Put yourself forward.

BIBLIOGRAPHY

1. James Strong, *The New Strong's Exhaustive Concordance of the Bible* (Nashville, TN: Thomas Nelson Publishers, 1990), ref. no. 4266.

2. Spiros Zodhiates, *The Complete Word Study Old Testament*, (Chattanooga, TN: AMG Publishers, 1994), ref. no. 4266.

3. Spiros Zodhiates, *The Complete Word Study New Testament*, (Chattanooga, TN: AMG Publishers, 1991), ref. no. 1411.

About Tim Sheets

Dr. Tim Sheets is an apostle, pastor, author, and founder of Awakening Now Prayer Network, based in Middletown, Ohio at the Oasis Church, which he has pastored for 36 years. He travels and ministers across the nation and other countries.

@TimDSheets (twitter)
Tim Sheets Ministries (facebook)

Write:

Tim Sheets Ministries
6927 Lefferson Road
Middletown, Ohio 45044

carol@timsheets.org

513.424.7150

timsheets.org
oasiswired.org
awakeningnowprayernetwork.com